TWAYNE'S WORLD AUTHORS SERIES

A Survey of the World's Literature

Sylvia E. Bowman, Indiana University

GENERAL EDITOR

RUSSIA

Nicholas P. Vaslef, U. S. Air Force Academy

EDITOR

Ivan Krylov

(TWAS 247)

TWAYNE'S WORLD AUTHORS SERIES (TWAS)

The purpose of TWAS is to survey the major writers —novelists, dramatists, historians, poets, philosophers, and critics—of the nations of the world. Among the national literatures covered are those of Australia, Canada, China, Eastern Europe, France, Germany, Greece, India, Italy, Japan, Latin America, the Netherlands, New Zealand, Poland, Russia, Scandinavia, Spain, and the African nations, as well as Hebrew, Yiddish, and Latin Classical literatures. To provide a truly international focus, foreign scholars have been invited to participate in the writing of these books. This survey is complemented by Twayne's United States Authors Series and English Authors Series.

The intent of each volume in these series is to present a critical-analytical study of the works of the writer; to include biographical and historical material that may be necessary for understanding, appreciation, and critical appraisal of the writer; and to present all material in clear, concise English—but not to vitiate the scholarly content of the work by doing so.

Ivan Krylov

By NIKOLAY STEPANOV

Nikolaĭ Leonidovich

Academy of Sciences of the USSR

Prepared for publication by the Novosti Press Agency (APN)
Publishing House, USSR

Twayne Publishers, Inc. :: New York

Preface

The names of the great fabulists of the past—Aesop, Phaedrus, La Fontaine, and Krylov—are established in world literature. Despite their national character, they are all examples of the best in fable writing, one of the oldest genres in the history of literature. Its roots can be traced back to beast epics and primitive mythology. This is particularly clearly seen in the Indian *Panchatantra* in which rudiments of the fable are still mingled with mythological narrative.

Aesop and Phaedrus perfected the genre of fable writing by breaking away from folklore and even turning it into a political weapon, often with a biting satirical plot. The fables of La Fontaine and Krylov were even more topical, commenting on contemporary events. With time, the topicality faded into the background and the most important feature of the fables became their universal worldly wisdom and common sense, born of the age-old experience of the people.

Krylov is the last in the dynasty of popular sages. The Russian writer, Nikolay Gogol, gave the most comprehensive definition of his fables, calling them "a book of the wisdom of the people themselves." This common sense gives Krylov's fables a permanent relevance and has made them part of Russian culture. This is not the limit of his role. Krylov, who was one of the creators of the Russian literary language, drew on the incalculable wealth of popular speech. Many lines and expressions from his fables have long been proverbs and sayings, and have become part of the everyday spoken language. His lavish verbal descriptions, his epigrammatical conciseness and precision, and the freshness and expressiveness of his figures of speech make his fables a constant source of delight.

Krylov holds a special place among Russian writers in that he is a popular poet, loved and understood both by young and adult readers. Gogol wrote:

He chose to walk along the least conspicuous and narrowest path, and walked along it almost noiselessly until he outgrew everyone else, just as a mighty oak outgrows the whole grove which had once concealed it. This poet is Krylov. He chose to write fables, a form neglected by all as old, useless, and something little more than child's play. But these fables made him a national poet.[1]

Many of us, both Russians and non-Russians, can remember how when we were children we recited to a gathering of other children and grownups Krylov's fable *The Crow and the Fox,* and how clearly we pictured the conceited Crow with its glossy black feathers and the tasty piece of cheese in its beak. Krylov's fables, with their comical animals, formed part of our childhood; they fascinated us and made us begin to understand the nature of good and evil, an understanding which has held good for life. But Krylov is not merely a children's writer. The wisdom of his fables can be appreciated to their full extent only after years of experience.

The narrow path Krylov chose turned out to be a felicitous and rewarding one. His fables made Russian literature aware of its robust national character. They depict the whole of Russia, from tsar to peasant. All classes, professions, and ranks are graphically and realistically portrayed in them. They provide a satirical picture of life and morals in Russia in the first half of the nineteenth century.

Contents

Chronology

1769   February 2 (13th New Style),* Ivan Krylov born in Moscow
        to Captain Andrey Prokhorovich and his wife, Maria Alexeevna
        Krylov.
1769-   Lives in Urals.
1774
1775   A. P. Krylov retires; family moves to Tver.
1775-   Lives in Tver.
1782
1778   Father dies. Young Krylov obtains employment at magistracy
        of Governor of Tver.
1782   Moves to St. Petersburg with mother and brother.
1783   September. Starts work as executive clerk at St. Petersburg
        Fiscal Board. Completes *Kofeynitsa* (The Coffee Fortune-
        teller), a comic opera in verse.
1784-   Ardent interest in theater. Meets actor, I. A. Dmitrevsky.
1785   Writes tragedy, *Cleopatra*.
1786   Writes *Philomela,* tragedy; and two comedies: *Beshenaya
        sem'ya* (The Mad Family) and *Sochinitel v prikhozhey* (The
        Writer in the Entry Hall). First appears in print in journal
        Lekarstvo ot skuki i zabot (A Cure for Boredom and Worries).
1787   May. Begins work in office of Mining Expedition. Mother dies.
1787-   Writes *Prokazniki* (The Mischevious Ones), a comedy, and
1788   libretto for opera, *Amerikantsy* (The Americans). Breaks with
        Ya. B. Knyazhnin, quarrels with Soymonov.
1789   Becomes friends with I. G. Rakhmaninov. January to August,
        publishes *Pochta dukhov* (The Spirits' Mail).
1791   December. Opens printing press and book stall. *I. Krylov
        sotovarishchi* (Krylov and Associates) (I. A. Dmitrevsky,
        P. A. Plavilshchikov and A. I. Klushin).
1792   Prints journal, *Zritel* (The Observer).
1793   Prints journal, *St. Petersburg Mercury.*
1797   Contributes to journal, *A Pleasant and Useful Way of Spend-
        ing the Time.*
1798-   Lives with Prince S. F. Golitsyn at his Kazatskoe estate as

---

* All the dates are given in the old style.

1800   Prince's secretary and tutor to his children.

1800   Writes *Podshchipa* (*Trumf*), a mock tragedy; stages it in private theater at Kazatskoe.

1800-   Writes *Pirog* (*The Pie*), a comedy. Moves to Riga as Prince
1801   Golitsyn's secretary.

1802   July 26. *The Pie* is staged in a Petersburg theater. Second printing of *Spirits' Mail*.

1803   September. Krylov leaves Prince Golitsyn's services and Riga.

1804   *The Pie* produced in Moscow.

1805   Takes up residence in Moscow. Writes first fables, translations of La Fontaine's *Oak and Reed* and *The Dainty Spinster*.

1806   Moves to Petersburg. Becomes a friend of the playwright Prince A. A. Shakhovskoy. July 27, the comedy *Modnaya lavka* (*The Fashion Shop*), is staged.

1807   In June writes and stages *Urok dochkam* (*A Lesson for Daughters*), a comedy. Writes fables: *Fox and Crow, A Little Box, Frog and Bullock, The Oracle, Hermit and Bear, The Peasant and Death.*

1807   Contributes to journal, *Dramatic Herald*. In October starts work in Finance Department.

1809   First publication of Krylov's fables in book form.

1811   Elected a member of the Russian Academy. *Ivan Krylov's Fables, a Revised Edition* and *New Fables by Ivan Krylov* are printed.

1812   January. Starts work at Imperial Public Library as assistant librarian in Russian Section. Reacts to events of Patriotic War of 1812 by writing fables, *Crow and Fowl, Sharing Up, The Wolf in the Kennels,* and *A Train of Carts.*

1815   Publication of *Ivan Krylov's Fables.*

1816   In March, promoted to librarian of Imperial Public Library. Elected active member of Moscow University Society of Lovers of Russian Literature.

1819   Publication of *I. A. Krylov's Fables* in six volumes.

1823   January. Awarded gold medal by Russian Academy for literary work.

1824   July 9. Journeys to Reval.

1825   Publication of *Ivan Krylov's Fables* in seven volumes.

1830   Publication of *Krylov's Fables* in eight volumes.

1834   Publication of two-volume edition of *Krylov's Fables* with illustrations by A. P. Sapozhnikov.

1838   Celebration of the Fiftieth Anniversary of Krylov's literary career.

Chronology

CHAPTER 1

The Life of Krylov

I Youth

IVAN Andreevich Krylov was born in Moscow on February 2 (13), 1769 into the family of an obscure army officer. His father, Andrey Krylov, a captain in the Orenburg dragoon regiment was not a member of the gentry, and in official documents styled himself "the son of an *ober-officer**.""[1] [*a subaltern officer]

Andrey Krylov spent many years as a private and then, as company clerk, quartermaster sergeant, and sergeant. As he had neither property nor a patron, he was promoted to ensign only after thirteen years—in 1764—and with great difficulty finally reached the rank of captain.

Krylov's father was involved in crushing the Pugachev uprising in 1773-75, and his family was in Orenburg when it was besieged by the rebelling peasants under Pugachev's leadership. In his *History of the Pugachev Rebellion,* Pushkin made use of a number of details about the blockade of Orenburg which he learned from Ivan Krylov. Mironov, in Pushkin's *The Captain's Daughter,* undoubtedly includes traits attributed to Andrey Krylov.

Ivan Krylov never forgot the time he spent in the Urals. Years later, he would still give lively accounts of the Ural Cossacks and tell about fishing in the winter.[2]

When the rebellion was quelled, Andrey Krylov, offended at not being decorated for his services, applied for a transfer from "military to civil service" on account of "weak health," and was "assigned to civil affairs."[3] In 1775 he was appointed president of the Tver district court of magistrates and moved with his family to the town of Tver.

Here the Krylovs lived a quiet provincial life: M. E. Lobanov, an intimate friend of the fabulist, writes that young Krylov

13

"learned to read and write in his parents' house, but he studied the elements of certain sciences and languages together with the children of family friends, the Lvovs." At home, his mother supervised his studies. "She was a simple woman," writes Lobanov, basing himself on Krylov's own account, "uneducated, but full of native wit . . ."[4]

Thanks to his new appointment, Krylov's father was able to introduce his family into Tver officialdom and gentry. Situated in the upper reaches of the Volga and halfway between Petersburg and Moscow, Tver was at that time a flourishing trading town. After the fire of 1763, its wooden houses were quickly replaced with stone ones. The cultural center was then the seminary in which town meetings took place. The seminarians also took an interest in literature and even published their own journal.

This quiet life did not last long. In 1778 Andrey Krylov died, leaving the family totally devoid of means of support.

Ivan's mother was forced to go out and make a living for the family by reciting prayers for the dead at homes of rich nobles and merchants. Testimony of the Krylovs' poverty has been preserved in the form of a petition for assistance by the widow, addressed to the Tsaritsa:

. . . Even though he was the son of an *oberofficer,* he had no ancestral lands or any other means of livelihood by which I could support myself and the children. He lived on his salary and nothing more; now that he is dead and I am left with two sons, one aged nine and the other one year old, I am at the mercy of all the cruel consequences of extreme poverty, and without the support of your Imperial Highness's generosity I shall be reduced to indescribable despair.[5]

The bereaved family, however, received no support. At the age of ten, Ivan Krylov was forced to serve as a clerk at the same chancellery in which his father had worked. This experience exposed young Krylov to the morals of provincial judges, the abuses of the bureaucracy, and the poverty of the old residents of Tver. In his adolescence, Krylov

took particular pleasure in mixing with people, going to the market square, watching swings and fist fights, rubbing shoulders with the colorful crowd, and avidly listening to their uneducated speech. He would sit for hours on the banks of the Volga near some washer-women and upon returning he would tell his friends the jokes and proverbs he heard the garrulous women relate.[6]

This knowledge of the people's customs and their racy spoken language can already be discerned in his first play *Kofeynitsa* (*The Coffee Fortune-teller*), but even more so in his fables.

Krylov did not receive a systematic education, which makes the reader marvel all the more at his erudition, wide range of interests, and knowledge of philosophy and literature which are already apparent in the plays and articles he wrote in the 1780's.

In the winter of 1782 he took a month's holiday and went with his mother and brother to Petersburg where his mother had petitioned for a pension. There he found work and decided to settle in the capital for good.

In Petersburg, Krylov worked for the Fiscal Board. It is not known whether he, his mother, and younger brother lived on her earnings or on the pittance he was paid for his office work, but when his mother died in 1788, he was left in charge of his brother.

Krylov had been attracted to the capital not only because of his dull life in Tver, but also because he wished to become a writer. Petersburg of the 1780's had an intensive cultural life: the Russian Academy, the first Russian theater, famous writers, new talent, exciting political views—all could be found here. The year Krylov came to Petersburg, Denis Fonvizin's comedy *Nedorosl* (*The Minor*) was staged for the first time. Fonvizin's merciless wit and the revolutionary writer Alexander N. Radi-shchev's truthfulness about the condition of the people in his *Puteshestvie iz Peterburga v Moskvu* (*Journey from Petersburg to Moscow*) represented the mental climate of progressive Rus-sia. This was the climate which formed young Krylov's world outlook; he was a passionate advocate of the Enlightenment, a penniless and titleless intellectual who had seen more than enough of the miserable life of the common people.

Krylov's first action in Petersburg was to try to have the libretto of his comic opera, *The Coffee Fortune-teller*, published.

He had written it on the basis of observations made in Tver at the age of fifteen. In Petersburg he heard of a printer named Breitkopf, a music connoisseur. He went straight to him with his first composition, asked him to set it to music, and to publish it. When Breitkopf offered him sixty rubles for the libretto, Krylov could hardly contain his excitement: this was the first reward for his youthful literary efforts. But his passion for reading was such that he asked to be paid in books instead of cash, and he was given works by Racine, Molière, and Boileau.[7] This first comedy never saw the light of day. But despite its literary naïveté, it contained the rudiments of his view of life and his sensibility to the realities of serf-owning Russia.

In Petersburg, too, Krylov developed a passion for the theater which tore him away from the milieu of minor officials and drew him into the world of actors and writers. At first he tried his hand at tragedy, but neither of the two historical tragedies he wrote at that time, *Cleopatra* and *Philomela* was staged, nor are they extant.

Not letting these failures discourage him, he wrote a series of comedies and comic opera librettos: *Beshenaya sem'ya*, (The Mad Family), *Sochinitel v prikhozhey* (The Writer in the Entry Hall and *Prokazniki* (The Mischievous Ones). He met P. A. Soymonov, a theater director and head of a mining expedition. In 1787, he started working at the mining office in charge of factories, but the theater remained Krylov's main interest.

Young Krylov was an impetuous fellow who had not yet learned to control his feelings and hide them under a mask of calm, ironic indifference. He was deeply hurt by the humiliation he had to suffer at the hand of theater directors who stubbornly refused to stage his plays despite their acknowledged merit. Meanwhile, he remained in dire financial straits—a titleless intellectual barely tolerated by the theater chiefs.

His impulsiveness led him to quarrel with Soymonov and the theater management. One of the main causes of this conflict was his play *The Mischievous Ones*, which was seen as a caricature of Yakov B. Knyazhnin, then considered an authority on play writing. Apart from matters of principle, personal resentment also played its part in the rift, which put an end to Krylov's career in the theater and to his hope of seeing his plays on the stage.

II *Meeting Progressives and Liberals*

In 1787, Krylov began to contribute regularly to I. G. Rakhmaninov's journals, *Lekarstvo ot skuki i zabot* (Medicine for Boredom and Troubles) and *Utrennie chasy* (Morning Hours). Its owner was a typical eighteenth-century freethinker of aristocratic origin, brought up on the philosophical ideas of the Age of Enlightenment. He translated Voltaire and Louis Sébastien Mercier, and was in close contact with the progressive, radically-minded Russian aristocratic intelligentsia, which idolized Radishchev.

Krylov's relationship with Rakhmaninov was important for the development of his ideas. Rakhmaninov was not only older and more experienced than Krylov, but was also well versed in philosophy, which undoubtedly affected the formation of Krylov's philosophical outlook.

At the beginning of 1789 an announcement in the *Moscow News* stated that bookshops were accepting subscriptions for a new monthly periodical, *Pochta dukhov* (The Spirits' Mail), "a learned, moral and critical correspondence of the Arab philosopher Mulikulmulk." The publisher, editor, and author of this monthly periodical was none other than Krylov.

It is noteworthy that the appearance of Radishchev's *Journey from Petersburg to Moscow* almost coincided with the publication of Krylov's *Spirits' Mail*. Although Krylov's journal for the most part confines itself to a satirical portrayal of the gentry and officialdom, and does not have the revolutionary tone of Radishchev's *Journey*, the two authors are linked by their sharp sentiments against the nobility.

The *Spirits' Mail* lasted hardly a year and had to close down in August, 1789, undoubtedly because of pressure on the part of the government. But Krylov did not abandon journalism, and even the banishment of Radishchev to a remote Siberian prison as punishment for publishing his *Journey* was not enough to frighten Krylov. In 1791, having conceived an idea for a new periodical, Krylov and his friends I. A. Dmitrevsky—an actor, P. A. Plavilshchikov—an actor and playwright, and A. I. Klushin —a writer, set up a joint printing press. This business was intended to be the same type of progressive establishment as N. I. Novikov's "Printing Company" had been some twenty years earlier. In a curious document, the contract of the four partners is pompously entitled: "The statutes on which the establishment of the printing press and the bookshop are based" and states that "this company bases itself on laws of genuine friendship."[8]

Having his own printing press and bookshop gave Krylov more independence and confidence. In 1792 Krylov and his friends produced a new periodical, *Zritel* (The Observer), a large part of which was devoted to the theater. The journal, the printing press, and the bookshop were not commercial enterprises, but were designed to bring together people with a common ideology. Dmitrevsky was an actor, Klushin came from an official milieu, while Plavilshchikov had a mercantile background. Their democratic ideas were strongly expressed in their writings. Plavilshchikov went to the Gymnasium attached to Moscow University, and after graduating in 1779, moved to Petersburg where he became an actor. He was one of the most consistent supporters of the idea for creating a Russian national theater. His comedies abound in descriptions of merchants and peasants. The fourth member of this literary association, Klushin, was also connected with the theater as a promising writer of comedies.

Ivan Krylov's intimacy with the "Voltairist" Rakhmaninov and the godless Klushin are clear evidence of prevailing sentiments. At the end of the eighteenth century in Russia, the term "Voltairist" applied not only to followers of Voltaire, but in general, to progressive and radical thinkers. Krylov's connection with Radishchev's group, is indicative of the fact that Krylov was mixing with the most progressive people of the period.

Russian "Voltairism" was a synonym for freethinking. It was not confined to witty, ironic scepticism about everything or to anticlerical enthusiasm. Russians who opposed autocratic despotism and the conservative role of religion studied Voltaire, as they did the other philosophers of the Enlightenment, as well as the Encyclopaedists and materialists, including Diderot, Rousseau, Helvétius, and Raynal.

What unified Krylov and his friends, and determined the ideological leaning of their journal was their support for the indigenous quality of Russian culture and the concept of patriotism which drew the *Observer* close to progressive members of the Russian Enlightenment, especially Fonvizin and Novikov.

Adherents of the Enlightenment in the 1760's and now *The Observer*, considered education to be the most important problem, and dealt with it in a patriotic spirit. The journal condemned the fashionable practice of entrusting the education of Russian children to foreign teachers. *The Observer* also continued the satire against nobility, started in the *Spirits' Mail*. "The right of the writer," reads an editorial from the publishers of the journal, "is to depict vice in all its foulness, so that each should feel repelled by it, and virtue in all its beauty, in order to captivate the reader with it. *The Observer* intends to indulge in this right." And indeed, it indulged in it fully. In the brilliant satirical lampoons published in the journal, Krylov exposed serfdom boldly, without pulling any punches.

Krylov's sentiments in those years are reflected in his poem "K Shchastiyu" (To Happiness) in which a poor honest man complains of Fortune's neglect, but who is not taken in by the tawdry fame of noble idlers. Krylov makes malicious fun of those who "raise themselves to the highest of fame with no intelligence, judgment, and honor, but by cunning, perfidy, and baseness." There is no doubt that this poem relates to his own life. When he writes that he stands "for truth," is "unloved by the nobility," and "persecuted because of truth," this is by no means a figure of speech. Krylov is referring to actual events: his quarrel with Soymonov and the theater managers, and the closing down of the *Spirits' Mail*.

The social atmosphere of those years was extremely tense: The Pugachev Rebellion was still within living memory; echoes of the French Revolution had reached the banks of the Neva; the government was combing the press for expressions of social discontent and taking steps to suppress them; Novikov was languishing in Schlusselburg Fortress; and Radishchev was in exile in Siberia. The wave of government repressions could not fail but to affect Krylov and his friends, for their journalistic and publishing endeavors had brought the displeasure of Catherine II upon them. On her instructions, in May 1792, the printing house of "Krylov and Associates" was searched for two essays by Krylov which are not extant: *Moi Goryachki* (My Feverish Haste) and *Gorlitsy* (Turtledoves) in which he expressed sympathy for the French Revolution. The searchers confiscated *Moi Goryachki* and handed it over to Catherine II.

This affair did not proceed further due to the absence of manifestly incriminating material, but Krylov and Klushin came under surveillance by the secret police and remained suspect for many years. After all these difficulties *The Observer* was closed down, but, in 1793, the persistent publishers initiated a new journal, the *Sankt-Peterburgsky Merkury* (The St. Petersburg Mercury); however, they were forced to take a more moderate position and to entrust the operation of the journal to others.

It is not known exactly how these "suspect" writers were prevented from publishing and writing, but Krylov—who was particularly compromised—not only had to abandon literature, but had to keep out of the way of the government for a long time.

III   *Travels*

From 1793 to 1801 Krylov wandered throughout the provinces. Appearing now and again at manor houses he knew, he led the nomadic existence of a man with no means or definite occupation.

Very little information has come down about his life during that period. He seems to have spent most of the time between 1793 and 1800 in the provinces, with frequent visits to Moscow. M. E. Lobanov, in his reminiscences, relates how Krylov visited Count Tatishchev at his estate. According to Lobanov, Krlyov "upon the departure of his host, having found himself alone on the estate" decided to experience the life of a primitive man, although this did not prevent him from "indulging in his ruling passion—reading."[9]

A most important stage in Krylov's life was his stay from 1798 to 1800 on Prince S. F. Golitsyn's estate in Kiev. Prince Sergey Golitsyn, a general, had distinguished himself in the Turkish campaign of 1791, but had been forced to retire by Emperor Paul I and live on his estate. His son, G. S. Golitsyn, was at first a general's aide-de-camp, but soon fell into disfavor, and upon retiring took up residence in his father's home. Thus, the entire family was in disgrace, and it was only natural that everyone at the estate strongly opposed Paul I and his regime. Krylov was given the post of secretary to S. F. Golitsyn and tutor to his children.

The young Krylov never ceased to amaze everyone with his range of gifts. In addition to his activities in literature, journalism, and the theater, he also acted, drew, and played the violin well. Krylov found in the Kazatskoe estate of the Golitsyns not only a refuge at a difficult period in his life, but a position which allowed him to keep his independence of opinion.

His views in those days are best illustrated by his comedy *Podshchipa* (Trumf) which was staged at Kazatskoe in February, 1800, at an amateur performance. Krylov played the part of the German Prince, Trumf. This mock-tragedy as a satire on Paul I and his war mania, and German dominance at the court.

Immediately after the palace coup and the death of Paul I in 1801, S. F. Golitsyn was appointed Governor-General of Riga. By a Senate order, Krylov was appointed to be his secretary on October 5, 1801, and in December 1802, was promoted to the rank of Provincial Secretary. On his way to Riga, Krylov stopped in Moscow and in Petersburg where he undertook a new edition of the *Spirits' Mail*. He stayed in Riga about two years and retired in 1802. At the end of 1803, Krylov went to Moscow where he stayed with his brother Lev, who was stationed with his regiment in Serpukhov, not far from Moscow. Krylov now settled down in Moscow, as evidenced by the production in a Moscow theater on January 25, 1804 of his comedy *Pirog* (The Pie).

In Moscow Krylov met I. I. Dmitriev, a most influential poet and widely known fabulist. Pyotr A. Pletnyov, Krylov's friend, noted the following:

As he wished to enter into relations with him which touch a subject they found equally diverting, Krylov spent his free time translating two of La Fontaine's fables: *The Oak and the Reed* and *The Fastidious Bride*. Dmitriev read them and "approved" of the translations, saying they were worthy of the delightful original.[10]

These first fables of Krylov appeared in the *Moskovsky Zritel* (Moscow Observer) of January, 1806.

IV *Years of Maturity*

Krylov was a contemporary of writers of the end of the eighteenth century such as Nikolay I. Novikov, Denis I. Fonvizin, Alexander N. Radishchev, Gavriil R. Derzhavin, and outlived Alexander S. Pushkin and the generation of Decembrists. Toward the end of his life he met writers of the 1840's, including Vissarion G. Belinsky and Ivan S. Turgenev.

After the turbulent years of his youth, he began a peaceful life upon his return to Petersburg in 1806, settling down to writing fables and devoting all his time and energy to this genre. He now valued peace and quiet, and for more than thirty years maintained a modest and unruffled mode of life.

Krylov's biography as a fabulist is usually reduced to a record of a few dates concerning his service and anecdotes illustrating his solitary and "lazy" existence. This is because there are no letters or memoirs which would have given us an insight into his inner life. His contemporaries had every reason to consider him a "riddle." The poet Konstantin N. Batyushkov, who knew him intimately, wrote to Nikolay I. Gnedich in 1809 that "Krylov was born an eccentric, but this eccentric is also a great riddle!"[11]

His later biographers distorted his image further by depicting him as indifferent and phlegmatic, isolated from social and literary life. But this was far from being true. He was a member of a number of literary and scholarly societies, and a frequent visitor to literary salons. He associated with the most distinguished writers of the time: Derzhavin, Zhukovsky, Batyushkov, Gnedich, Griboedov, Shakhovskoy, and later—Pushkin. His writing was now more restrained and guarded, and by no means did he express all his thoughts. His former troubles, his forced abandonment of literature, and his years of wandering had left their mark on him. The tragic fates of the liberals, Radishchev and Novikov and their cruel persecution by the tsarist régime, were an object lesson for him.

Krylov changed in many respects: He became a closed person and hid his innermost thoughts. The guise of eccentricity and laziness that was recorded by his contemporaries was a defense to protect himself from idle—though not infrequently importunate and suspicious—curiosity.

This image of a lazy, genial, and ironic man who seemed to stand to one side of current events made it easier for Krylov to express his real opinion of society in his fables. His position was neither that of the conservative landowners nor that of the liberal Decembrists, which explains to a large degree why he was such a riddle to his contemporaries.

Krylov did not devote himself to fables immediately upon his return to the capital, but began writing plays again, working on his comedies, *Modnaya lavka* (The Fashion Shop) and *Urok dochkam* (A Lesson for Daughters). He now became a friend of the distinguished playwright, Prince Alexander A. Shakhovskoy, a supporter of Classical traditions adapted to the national idiom. In 1803, together with Shakhovskoy and Alexander I. Pisarev, Krylov took part in the publication of the journal, *Dramatichesky vestnik* (The Dramatic Herald), which regularly featured his new fables. *The Dramatic Herald* advocated a typically Russian style in literature and to a certain degree upheld the traditions of *The Observer* and *The Petersburg Mercury*. It welcomed writing which displayed knowledge of "the customs, speech, mentality, feelings, and morals of the Russian people."[12]

From the beginning of 1807, Krylov went to literary gatherings at the house of Admiral Alexander S. Shishkov, a Classicist, which soon turned into a permanent literary society attracting mostly Classicists opposing Sentimentalism. On the eve of the Napoleonic wars, at the beginning of 1811, this society was officially known as *Beseda Lyubiteley Russkogo Slova* (Society of the Lovers of the Russian Word), and Krylov became one of its members. *The Society* was a conservative establishment, and

the patriotic sentiments of its members, as well as its "popular
character"—idealizing obsolete patriarchal aspects in the lives
of the common people—gave it a reactionary tinge.

During its last years of existence (1813 to 1816) *The Society*
lost almost all its social and literary importance and became a
target for derisive attacks by the new generation of writers
united around a circle of friends of the Romantic Vasily A.
Zhukovsky. This circle later became the literary group called
"Arzamas," which was opposed to *The Society* of Admiral Shishkov.

Krylov, however, was in a special, independent position in
The Society, by no means fully sharing either its political views
or its passion for restoring Classicism. He regarded the national
culture not from the point of view of preserving its patriarchal,
serf-owning basis, as did Shishkov, but as something belonging
to all the people. Evidence of his disapproval of *The Society*
can be found in the fable, *Statesman and Thinker* (1815), directed
at one of its most active members, Count Dmitry I. Khvostov,
a giftless graphomaniac. *Demyan's Fish Soup* (1813) was a
satirical comment on the long and boring speeches at *The Society*. His friend M. E. Lobanov relates how, having promised
to read one of his latest fables, Krylov once arrived at a *Society*
meeting rather late. Someone was reading an extraordinarily long
play. The audience was weary and beginning to get bored; many
could not help yawning. Then Krylov read his fable. Lobanov
recalls that its content was amazingly appropriate to the situation and its application so apt and to the point that the audience
rewarded the author with loud, heartfelt laughter.[13]

Despite his success as a fabulist, Krylov's return to literature was by no means as easy as it might have been. The fact
that he had written bold satire to which the state had objected
was not forgotten. His failure to be elected to the Russian Academy (a society for the study of Russian language and literature)
in 1809 could have been the result of the government's displeasure. When, two years later, he was elected a member, he
played little part in its activities, mainly because Shishkov and
his group held important positions in the Academy, and Krylov
neither liked nor trusted them.

At the beginning of 1809, Krylov's first book of fables was printed, bringing him national fame. From that time on he spent nearly twenty-five years writing fables. He became more popular with every passing year and his public readings of new fables were literary events. One contemporary wrote:

The effect produced by his minute compositions was unbelievable: there were often no seats left in the hall; visitors crowded around the poet, and stood on chairs, tables, and window ledges, for fear of missing one word.[14]

Individual expressions from his fables were quickly picked up, many becoming proverbs.

When the Public Library (now the Saltykov-Shchedrin State Library) was organized in 1812, Krylov was given a position there through the influence of the director, A. N. Olenin. The library was actually opened in 1814. Olenin, a highly cultured official, was influential at the court. He had been elected a member of the Russian Academy as early as 1786 and Krylov had met him in the 1790's. Olenin was associated with Derzhavin's circle and was a friend of Ivan I. Khemnitser, the fabulist and other writers. Krylov became a regular guest at his house.[15] For many years Olenin was Krylov's patron, not only helping him through everyday adversities, but keeping a careful watch over his literary activities.

Olenin's concern was to attract representatives of various social opinions and literary tastes. Unlike the exclusiveness of Shishkov's *Society*, Olenin's drawing room was a center for different views and schools: "Literary and artistic subjects occupied and animated the conversation; complete freedom of treatment, unrestrained frankness, the good-natured reception of the hosts—all this lent a patriarchal, family atmosphere to the circle . . ."[16]

Anna Kern, one of Pushkin's friends, described one such evening:

I did not notice [Pushkin] at first, so engrossed was I in the charades that were being performed by Krylov, Pleshcheev, and others. I cannot quite remember why, but Krylov was made to pay a forfeit by reciting one of his fables. He sat down on a chair in the middle of the room; we all crowded round him; and I shall never forget what a fine figure he cut as he read [his fable] the *Ass!* And even now I sometimes hear his voice and imagine his intelligent face and the comic expression with which he uttered: "An ass more honest ne'er existed!"[17]

Krylov frequented Olenin's drawing room together with Push-kin, Zhukovsky, Batyushkov, Gnedich, and other writers hostile to *The Society*.

Olenin was a clever and influential courtier and not only acted as Krylov's benevolent patron, but laid claim to directing his work. On a number of occasions he suggested themes for the fables and kept an eye on Krylov's development, performing the role of a friendly, but at the same time fairly severe, semi-official political and ideological censor. Apart from suggesting themes he would often suggest the morals, too, with which Krylov rarely agreed. Fables such as *The Pearl Divers, Author and Robber, Horse and Rider,* and *The Godless Tribe* were undoubtedly written either under Olenin's influence or at his direct command.

In 1819 the third, supplemented, edition of Krylov's fables came out. Between 1820 and 1823 he wrote thirty fables which appeared in print in 1825, in a fourth edition of his collected fables. The reason for the silence between the two editions was illness. In 1823 he suffered two paralytic attacks, and the state of his health became a cause of general concern. The court also became worried about his state of health and offered him the use of Pavlovsk, the Tsarina's palace, in which to recuperate.

Krylov took thirty years to write not more than two hundred fables, most of which are masterpieces of literary skill, delightful in their originality and vividness.

A great part of his life was taken up by work at the Public Library. Recently discovered business letters and memoranda in the library archives prove that he worked conscientiously there, displaying great initiative and energy.

In addition to Krylov, other famous writers and bibliographers recruited by Olenin worked in the Library. Apart from Krylov and Gnedich, N. A. Vostokov, Baron Anton A. Delvig, M. Lob-anov, and Mikhail N. Zagoskin all helped give the Library a liter-

ary aura.[18] The dossier on his work shows that Krylov did a great
deal of bibliographical work, in addition to classifying prints
and having other duties.

Krylov was also responsible for the acquisition of Russian
books in the Library. When he started work there, the total
number of Russian book titles was four, but by 1820 it was
more than 10,000.[19] Evidence of his work can be found in *I. A.
Krylov's Memorandum on Cataloging the Books of the Imperial
Library, dated 25 May, 1818.*[20]

Krylov spent a number of years compiling a catalog of recom-
mended books in all branches of knowledge. This major work,
entitled *A Bibliographical-Alphabetical Index Composed by Ivan
Andreevich Krylov, Librarian at the Imperial Public Library,*
consists of almost three thousand titles of books on philosophy,
law, physics, chemistry, literature (titled "Oratory" and "Verse
Writing"). He devoted a particularly large section to fables. Of
his own books, besides the various editions of his fables,
he included *The Fashion Shop* and *A Lesson for Daughters.*[21]
His closest associates for a number of years were the famous
Russian bibliographer V. Sopikov, and later Delvig, the poet.

V *Philosophical Laziness?*

In the 1830's Krylov, now in his sixties, found it difficult to
fulfill his duties at the Library. This explains the following
event, recorded by his colleague I. Bystrov: "Krylov was now
old, corpulent, and sluggish. I kept finding him sleeping like a
log on the divan. I had to wait for the watchman to wake him,
and he would get up grumbling, take a long time over finding
the book, and hand it over not altogether amiably."[22]

Even though he had now attained fame, he did not change
his simple way of life and devoted all his time and energy to
writing. He lived in a small flat in the Library building. He
mostly sat at home in his dressing gown on a divan in a corner
room which looked out on the Gostinny Court. He rarely left the
house except to go to work at the Library, dine at the English
Club, or visit the Olenin household in the evenings. He often
spent the summer at the Olenins' country house in Priyutino,

near Petersburg, to which all the Library and the entire Petersburg literary world came for visits throughout the year. In
the summer the atmosphere in Priyutino was gay and relaxed.
Literary evenings and shows were held. F. Oom writes:

Krylov, Shakhovskoy, and Gnedich competed with one another for
the best compositions on these occasions and Priyutino was used
as the normal place for first performances of plays by famous authors.
. . . Krylov spent the whole summer here: he was given accommoda-
tion in an attractive house called "Banya," surrounded by a garden
on a hill.[23]

Konstantin Batyushkov described Krylov as a philosopher-poet,
a serene sage in the quiet of the "Priyutino woods." He understood that under Krylov's disguise of laziness and eccentricity
lay a wise attitude toward life, giving him a deep understanding of that life:

> A happy, lazy poet,
> And shrewd philosopher,
> Krylov stands in the shade of birch,
> And beasts of fancy watch him think
> Them up.
> He plucks Parnassus' rose
> In Priyutino woods.[24]

Krylov's years of wandering taught him much. His wisdom
stemmed from bitter experience. He was no longer the inde-
fatigable journalist, publisher, and playwright who applied all
his ebullient energy to whatever business was at hand. He now
strove to keep his personal freedom intact and insure an independence of thought which was difficult to maintain even in
the Aesopic language of the fables. This to a certain extent
refutes the legendary reputation of the phlegmatic "eccentric
and lazy fellow," a reputation which was already crystallizing
at the beginning of the nineteenth century. This reputation made
it possible for him to preserve his independence, brush aside
importunate friends, and guard himself from the suspicion and
watchful attention of the government. He, therefore, did everything to make people think that he was a sage "lying in philo-
sophic dream."

In his daily life and habits he deliberately emphasized his indifference to the vanity and luxury of the society around him. Lobanov, who knew him well, writes: "In the morning and evening he was always to be found in a dilapidated dressing gown and sometimes just in his night shirt, barefooted or wearing slippers, sitting on a stained divan worn by his weight, a cigarette in one hand and a book in the other."[25] This, however, did not mean that Krylov refused to keep up with current events or that he had no ideological or creative life. It was typical of him not to try to disprove these rumors; they were his shield. Even Pushkin included in his *Table Talk* an amusing anecdote about Krylov's philosophical sloth:

Above the divan where Krylov usually sat at home, hung a large picture in a heavy frame. Someone pointed out to him that the nail on which it hung was not firmly fixed and that it could break off some day and kill him. "No," Krylov answered, "in that case the angle of the frame will certainly have to describe an oblique line and miss my head."[26]

This good-natured joke illustrates Krylov's light-heartedness and his attachment to an established pattern of life, and perhaps even his love of mathematics, which he studied with interest.

Despite his great mental agility Krylov remained in many respects a man of the eighteenth century—a progressive Voltairist. He retained his views on natural law and on education as a force which determines a man's moral and civic make-up. He had a clear and rational cast of mind. His literary sympathies and taste showed that he supported Classicism to a considerable extent. This of course was very much out of date at a time when Romanticism in literature was asserting itself more and more forcefully and when the philosophy of the German idealist Friedrich Schelling was on everyone's lips. Krylov, however, did not limit himself to a narrow circle of people who held the same literary views; he gladly attended informal gatherings at his friends' homes, as well as the literary salons of his literary opponents.

Krylov was immutably true to the literary genre he had chosen, even though he himself effected a revolution within this form,

bringing it closer to life and turning it into a Realistic form of
art. This is why the founders of Russian Realistic literature—Pushkin, Gogol, and Belinsky—were so delighted with his fables.

The poet, Pyotr A. Vyazemsky, had a better understanding
than the rest of his contemporaries of the deliberateness of his
behavior:

Krylov was by no means a lighthearted, scatterbrained and childishly
careless La Fontaine, as we are wont to think. . . . Whatever he did,
he did with extraordinary intelligence. . . . Fables were his calling
not only because of the innate gifts that he himself seemed not to
suspect he possessed, but also as a result of his learning in a stern
school of life. In the fables he could be totally cunning and say much
without letting the cat out of the bag; he could use animals to touch
upon problems, circumstances, and personalities which perhaps he
was not brave enough to mention openly.[27]

When he was fifty Krylov learned ancient Greek, and English
at the age of fifty-three. He learned ancient Greek for the
express purpose of reading Homer in the original and he himself translated a passage of the *Odyssey* and read the principal
Greek classics including Aesop's fables.[28] This was noted by
Pushkin when he refuted the French critic Lemontey's claim
that Krylov knew no foreign language:

. . . Krylov knows the most important European languages, and aside
from that, like Alfieri, he learned ancient Greek at the age of fifty.
In other countries, such an accomplishment by a famous figure
would be in the newspapers, but we are content to let biographies
of our famous writers list their dates of birth and details of their
service record.[29]

Pushkin was, thus, the first to explode the myth of Krylov's
laziness and general indifference.

Even in his old age Krylov did not lose his quick mind and
biting wit. The Polish poet, Adam Mickiewicz, "was in rap-
tures over Krylov's wit and loved to repeat the anecdotes and
words in which the Russian fabulist expressed himself so well.
In short, he considered that Krylov personally was greater than
his reputation as a writer."[30]

Krylov's skillful and expressive readings were a sort of

dramatization of his fables and always attracted large audiences. At the same time he did not shun the society of the future revolutionaries—the Decembrists. In the early 1820's he willingly published his fables in Kondrati F. Ryleev's and Alexander A. Bestuzhev's *Polyarnaya zvezda* (Polar Star) and gave energetic assistance to *Sorevnovatel prosveshcheniya* (Challenge of Education), the organ of the *Free Society of Lovers of Russian Literature*. In the *Sorevnovatel* Krylov published his fable about the tsar's censorship, *Cat and Nightingale,* as well as his stinging— though softened to meet the requirements of the authorities— *Fishes Dancing* which was reprinted in *Polar Star.* In 1823 the *Polar Star* printed *Peasant and Sheep,* which the critic Vissarion Belinsky later used as an example of Krylov's socially-orientated satire.

One must not, however, exaggerate the importance of these facts and compare Krylov's political position with that of the Decembrists. Though Krylov by no means identified himself with the Decembrists, he followed their activities with interest and they in turn sympathized with him. Krylov, indeed, evinced such great concern for their uprising on December 14, 1825 that he spent almost the entire day on Senate Square where it took place, thus breaking with his customary immobility.

Following the abortive revolt of the Decembrists, society entered a new period. As Alexander I. Herzen wrote: "The surface of official Russia—the show Empire—showed only losses, a savage reaction, inhuman persecutions, and an intensification of despotism."[31] Krylov, too, was affected by this change. Remote as he was from the Decembrists' political aims, he did not take the revolutionary event of December 14, 1825 as the collapse of his ideals. On the contrary, this strengthened his conviction that the situation in the country could not be righted by revolutionary means. Krylov did not alter his secret opposition or his ironic attitude to the system—the "barracks and offices"— which, in Herzen's words, had become the support of Nicholas I's autocracy, but he had to hide his opposition more deeply, both in his private and social life.

Although Krylov had a distrustful and ironic attitude toward the nobles and officials, he still did not isolate himself, as evi-

denced by his attendance at various literary evenings. For example, he met Pushkin and others often at Zhukovsky's Saturday gatherings.[32] Pletnyov mentions Pushkin, Gnedich, and
Batyushkov as being present at these gatherings and writes:

Krylov, too, used to attend as everybody's friend. His practical
intelligence and fine understanding always found much food for
thought independently of the enjoyable entertainment he could
derive from the medley of visitors who all loved him equally. At
Zhukovsky's Saturday gatherings he gave noticeably freer vent to
his wit and amiability; the absence of ladies, the reading of literary
news, and the easy atmosphere loosened his customary guardedness.[33]

VI *Old Age*

As the years passed, Krylov's literary activity diminished and
he produced only two or three fables a year. He was very strict
with himself, his worst fear being that he would exhaust his
inspiration. Thus, in a letter dated 1829 to his friend V. A.
Olenina, he informed her that he had sent her three new fables
and added: "Read my fables and tell me honestly: have I become
much more stupid, and how do they compare with my earlier
ones? Oh, how I am afraid of becoming like the Archbishop of
Granada and of being told: 'Point d'homélies, Monseigneur.' "[34]

Krylov's fears were groundless; his fables kept their clarity of
thought and formal perfection till the end. In 1834, the last year
of his literary life, he wrote *Cock and Cuckoo* and *A Great Lord*
which fittingly ended his literary career. In the last ten years
of his life he continued to frequent literary gatherings and societies, but no longer took any part in literary activities.

The image of Krylov preserved by his contemporaries belongs
to his last years, when he had stopped writing fables. This
paunchy, clever, playfully good-natured Krylov, ironically indifferent to the world around him had already outlasted the
years of his literary activities and had outlived his contemporaries. In a distinctive literary portrait of the old fabulist, Ivan
Turgenev conveys his elusive irony:

I met Krylov only once, at a party held by a high-ranking though
untalented Petersburg writer. He sat for two or three hours or more,

immobile, between two windows. If only he would utter a word! He wore a loose, shabby tail-coat and a white neckerchief; his stout legs were enveloped in tasseled boots. He leaned with both hands on his knees and did not even turn his colossal, heavy, and stately head; only his eyes occasionally moved under their beetle-brows. One could not tell whether he was listening and observing silently, or just sitting and existing. There was neither sleepiness nor attention on that broad, purely Russian face, but only boundless intelligence . . . and an old man's laziness; and now and again it seemed as if something playful wanted to come out and could not—or did not want to—force its way through all that senile fat.[35]

On February 2, 1838, Krylov's seventieth birthday and the fiftieth anniversary of his literary career were celebrated, though, in fact, the latter did not coincide with this date. (*The Coffee Fortune-teller* was written in 1783 and Krylov was first published in 1786.) In allowing these celebrations, the government wanted to make up for the negative impression caused by Pushkin's tragic death by displaying concern for the country's literature. It, therefore, tried to make the occasion an official one and to strictly regulate it. Nevertheless, the celebrations had wide social repercussions. Zhukovsky made a speech in which he said: "Though few of us have gathered here, the anniversary we are celebrating is a national event; if it had been possible to involve the whole of Russia in it, she would have taken part with the same feeling as is alive in all of us this minute." Despite an official ban, Zhukovsky mentioned Pushkin's death in his speech, saying that he had been "abducted from the hopes his genius had evoked in his native land."[36] After the celebration speeches, a cantata was sung in the fabulist's honor, after which he was strewn with flowers and laurel wreaths.

After having worked for thirty years in the Public Library, Krylov retired in March, 1841, at the age of seventy-two. A draft of a report he wrote says: "Owing to poor health and old age, he feels that he cannot fulfill his duties as he ought to and as he would wish to. . . ."[37] Upon retirement, Krylov moved to a quiet flat on Vasilevsky Island in Petersburg. He adopted his goddaughter's family and they lived with him. He spent his time with them, teaching the children to read and write, and

listened to their music lessons. He was happy when children
played near him.

In 1841 Krylov was elected academician at the newly organized Russian Language and Literature Department of the
Academy of Sciences. His last task was to prepare a full edition
of his fables for print in 1843. On November 21, 1844 he died
at the age of seventy-five, and was buried in the Alexander
Nevsky Monastery next to his friends Gnedich and Nikolay M.
Karamzin. In 1855 a nationwide collection was held to build
a memorial to him in the Summer Garden. This celebrated
memorial by P. Klodt shows a massive figure with big peasant
hands, a massive head, and a corpulent torso. The whole appearance suggests a Russian peasant's firmness. Even his portrait
painted by the famous Russian artist K. Bryullov shortly before
his death, gives the impression that he had arrayed himself in
a tail-coat with a star and had spruced himself up especially
for the occasion. Neither the tail-coat nor the star suit him
well—this wise, democratic, "grandfather Krylov," a simple man
from a simple background. His unostentatious life and, most
important, his peasantlike, playful common sense, had turned
the fabulist into a true national sage.

CHAPTER 2

A Writer of the Eighteenth Century

I *The Shaping of his World Outlook*

IVAN Krylov's main literary output consisted of fables. They
show with particular clarity his genius and his calling as
a satirist. But before he turned to fable writing, he had already
gone through a long and complicated literary life. He was a
noted writer of comedies at the end of the eighteenth century,
and had written brilliant satire in journals, as well as original,
vivid lyric poetry. When he started writing fables he found the
genre in which he could make use of all his previous experience.
There is no doubt about the close links between his fables and
his plays and satire.

The Classicism of the nobility favored such "high" genres
as the ode, the epic, and the tragedy, for they served to glorify
the might and majesty of the noble estate. But, alongside this
prevailing literary movement, beginning in the second half of
the eighteenth century, Realistic influences began making inroads.
These trends came from those democratic elements which opposed Feudalism. The satirical writings of Prince Antioch D.
Kantemir, Denis Fonvizin, and Gavriil Derzhavin displayed the
type of attitude to reality that motivated Krylov to try to continue
this satirical trend.

The activity of such outstanding publicists and writers as
Nikolay Novikov, Denis Fonvizin, and Mikhail D. Chulkov expressed the progressive tendencies in Russian social thought and
literature in the second half of the eighteenth century, the most
powerful exponent of which was Alexander Radishchev's revolutionary homily, *Journey from Petersburg to Moscow.* This work
went beyond the program of the Enlightenment; it raised the

35

question, for the first time in Russian literature, of the peasant
revolution and dealt harshly with all the ideological, legal, and
economic foundations of the autocratic, serf-owning system.
The *Journey* describes, in a raw and authentic manner, the
oppression and cruelty of the landowners towards their serfs
and the arbitrary rule of the entire tsarist bureaucratic apparatus.

Progressive Russian thought, in contrast to Western European
thought, was associated not with the activity of the bourgeoisie—
which was not a revolutionary class in Russia—but above all,
with the people's and the peasants' movements. Moreover, it
was not sheltered from Western European Enlightenment and
revolutionary ideas, avidly absorbing everything new and progressive advocated by outstanding Western thinkers. Russian
publicists and writers were thoroughly familiar with the works
of Voltaire, Rousseau, Locke, Ferguson, Mably, Raynal, Diderot,
Helvétius, Montesquieu, and Holbach.

This progressive trend in Russian thought and literature was
marked primarily by a hostile attitude to the ideology of the
aristocracy and its presence in culture and everyday life and,
secondly, by sharp criticism of Gallomania—a repudiation by the
ruling circles of their national heritage. Other features included
its tendencies toward materialist thought, its protest against the
religious and clerical nature of the philosophical and moral basis
of feudalism, and a striving for realism in the representation of
life in art. The satirical genres—journalism, comedy, and fables—
portrayed contemporary Russian life with the greatest veracity.

In forming his *Weltanschauung*, young Krylov was influenced
by major revolutionary events in Russia and in Western Europe:
the peasant uprising led by Pugachev and the French Revolution.
By the end of the eighteenth century, progressive forces were
growing in Russian society, antifeudal sentiments were gaining
force, bold voices in defense of the people could be heard with
increasing frequency, and progressive, independent works were
being published exposing the autocratic, serf-owning system.
The highlight of this revolutionary, democratic thought were
the works of Alexander Radishchev who gave a wonderfully apt
description of those turbulent times in his ode, *The Eighteenth
Century*:

> Oh signal century! To happy mortals
> You grant the gift of truth and liberty
> And light: the eternal constellation bright.[1]

It was under this constellation of "truth" and "freedom" that young Krylov developed his various and brilliant talents. He was one of the most notable writers of the eighteenth century whose name was associated with those of Novikov and Radishchev.

In his youth, Krylov continued the tradition of writers of the Enlightenment—Antioch Kantemir, Mikhail V. Lomonosov, Nikolay Novikov, and Denis Fonvizin. They had repudiated the old, feudal system and had believed in the possibility of settling the main problems of the social structure by means of reason. The ideas of the Enlightenment were also expressed in Classicist literature which was largely based on a rationalistic system of thought. In those works which he wrote in the eighteenth century—his comedies and satire (*Spirits' Mail* and *Kaib*)—Krylov had already gone beyond the bounds of Classicist rationalism. He abandoned abstract structures and began depicting life as it was, writing satire and biting critical essays. His characters Rhymestealer, Mrs. Modey, Hopskip, Mrs. Take-me and Mrs. Shameless—are taken from life and are not Classical Comedy stereotypes. He depicts characters who have been molded by their environment and their social milieu, which lends realism to his comedies and satire, and makes his characters a part of real life.

These stylistic traits are found in a more pronounced form in his fables. In fact, his first fables were published in Rakhmaninov's journal, *Utrennie chasy* (Morning Hours), in 1788. They were published anonymously, but we know they are Krylov's because of the discovery in 1900 of an editor's copy of the journal in which the authors' names are written. Krylov himself never laid claim to his first four fables. Their subject matter is similar to the satire in the *Spirits' Mail.*

His bitter experience as a penniless official, a typical titleless intellectual of that period, led him to emphatic repudiation of aristocratic society, as can already be seen in the writings of his youth. The maturity and erudition manifested in his early writings are truly amazing. He did not offer his talents to the court, as did the majority of unprincipled writers. However, in his youth, his political views were not as independent or consistent as Radishchev's. Krylov accepted the main political ideas of the eighteenth century: justice and the rule of law, the harmfulness of despotism, Enlightenment as a force which reeducates people, the natural equality of people, and the injustice of estate privileges. Krylov's merit lies not in putting forth new ideas, but in adapting them to Russian life by illustrating them with actual national images and colors. This is what made him one of the founders of Russian Realistic literature.

The literature of the eighteenth century was to a great extent didactic. It strove to establish rules of conduct and advocated a morality which fought depravity and the social injustice of the feudal system. The concepts of "reason" and "virtue" were the cornerstones of the social philosophy of the Enlightenment. In his course on *The History of Russian Literature,* Maxim Gorky wrote: "The fact that literature was looked at—from an educational point of view—as a means of improving morals and training man, is confirmed by the preference for comedies which criticized morals to other types of literature and the enormous number of translated and original fables."[2] And this is how young Krylov began his literary activity, with comedies on morals and manners, publicistic satire, and fables; in short, with the genres conditioned by the educational function of literature.

II *Playwriting*

Krylov settled on fables after passing through the genres of comedy and satire. Comedy taught him to depict real life and shape the typical and expressive natures of the characters in his fables. His comedies and satires contained the themes and motifs which he subsequently expanded in his fables.

Krylov's comedies occupy an important place, not only in his works, but in the history of the Russian theater. They are a part of the same group as Fonvizin's comedies *Nedorosl* (*The Minor*) and *Brigadir* (*The Brigadier*). Krylov's plays fall short of Fonvizin's in broadness of social scope and realism, but they stand out from among the works of many writers of the late eighteenth century because of their democratic leanings, and mark an important stage in the history of Russian comedy. His comedies retain much of Molière's precepts on the grotesque farce in comedies, but are imbued with topical humor, accurate observations, and sarcasm.

Together with Alexander P. Sumarokov, Denis Fonvizin, and Yakov Knyazhnin, Krylov was one of the founders of Russian comedy which reached its peak in the nineteenth century in the works of Nikolay V. Gogol and Alexander N. Ostrovsky. In his comedies, Krylov mocks the moral depravity of typical representatives of St. Petersburg's aristocracy. This was a perennial theme in comedies and in satirical journalism in the second half of the eighteenth century, but Krylov was more successful than his forerunners in making his characters true to life. His main accomplishment was to create a free and expressive language and racy dialogue. Krylov's comedies sparkle with real humor and lively, colloquial dialogue—a refreshing change from the ponderous language of most comedies of that century.

The Coffee Fortune-teller already has the social theme that was to become the main theme of his plays and journalistic satire. The typically frivolous, dissolute, stupid, and willful estate owner, Novomodova (Mrs. Modey), appears in one form or another in almost all his plays. His early comedies boldly dealt with the matter of the landlord's cruelty and the plight of the peasant serf. Mrs. Modey breaks up the happiness of two young lovers by forcing her serf girl to marry the steward, and accuses the girl's betrothed of theft, sending him to the army. In the end, the lovers overcome all obstacles and are reunited, but the angry attack on the serf system makes this early work of Krylov's very characteristic of all his later writings.

The early tragedy, *Philomela*, also points to Krylov's political views and sentiments. Written in 1786, it occupies a much more important place in his works than is commonly supposed by those who consider it a casual and unsuccessful youthful experiment.

Tragedy, however, was not Krylov's forte, and he tried his

hand at other genres—satire, comedy, lyric poetry, and prose. After *Philomela* he returned to comedy, with which he felt much more at ease.[3] That same year, 1786, he wrote the opera *Beshenaya sem'ya* (*The Mad Family*) in the spirit of the comic operas of the end of the eighteenth century with their rather coarse humor reminiscent of Sumarokov's farces. The comedy *Sochinitel v prikhozhey* (*Writer in the Entry Hall*) (1786) was more significant and independent in conception. It mocks the venal, obsequious poets who wrote flattering odes and madrigals on every possible occasion for their noble patrons. This comedy reveals Krylov's particular talent for playwriting. It has an easy, free style, and is full of wit and youthful good spirits. The empty-headed, mincing coquette, Mrs. Modey, who keeps a visitors' book for her lovers and dupes the enamored Count Dullard; her sly confidante, the maid Dasha; and the obsequious Rhymestealer—are not merely conventional comic characters, as in *The Mad Family*, but are characters from real life.

In many respects Krylov's comedies are derived from Molière. They are comedies of intrigue, abounding in farce, with deft, quick-witted servants arranging their masters' affairs. But behind this structure, Krylov's plays contain a topical and sharply satirical theme. Real life is even more apparent in the comedy *Prokazniki* (*The Mischievous Ones*), in which he ridicules the playwright Knyazhnin, thinly-veiled as the character Rhymestealer, whom he denounces for slavish imitation of French writers, particularly Racine and Voltaire. The play has a traditional plot—two lovers overcome the obstacles preventing their union—but its main content, distinguishing it from other plays, is a literary polemic against Classicist tragedy. He advocates national originality in Russian playwriting and draws a caricature of the narcissistic poet Rifmokrad (Rhymestealer) accusing him of having contempt for his national culture.

Krylov largely succeeded in creating the figure of the absent-minded Rhymestealer, totally involved in his literary activities and not noticing what is going on in his own house. His sharply satirical digs at Knyazhnin were easily detected by his contemporaries; for this reason the play was banned and never staged. Apart from this, the play is full of realistic details and images scrupulously taken from life. This realistic treatment of life singled Krylov out from among his contemporaries.

The Mischievous Ones is above all a literary lampoon maliciously parodying poets who slavishly imitate foreign culture. At the same time Krylov had specific facts in mind when he portrayed characteristic aspects of the period and its literature. Although his comedy is full of sharp polemics against Knyazhnin, a favorite writer of the court, the essential thing in the play is Krylov's treatment of topical material and his ability to overcome the abstract and rationalistic typology characteristic of Classical eighteenth-century comedies.

Although he observed the principles of the three unities— place, time, and action—Krylov was interested in making his play true to life. He justified particular features of his comedy and objected to the pedantic demands of writers of the Classicist school that humor and pathos should be separated. The importance of Krylov's comedies is not in the artfully constructed plots—which boil down to the happy reunion of lovers—but in the plausibility of the characters. Still, they were not typical enough and had not yet become real people. Krylov seems to have stopped midway: the realistic principles he had contemplated were implemented by him later in his fables.

Krylov was not alone in writing comedies about common people. He was, in fact, outdone by his friend and fellow-editor of *The Observer*, Pyotr Plavilshchikov, whose comedies *Sidelets* (*The Sitter*) and *Bobyl'* (*The Widower*) recreate the lives of Russian merchants and peasants, and in many respects are close to Krylov's scenes from everyday life. Plavilshchikov attached great importance to comedies and explained that the writer's task was to "tell the truth while making people laugh." "The task of comedy is to expose vice in such a way that the man who recognizes himself in this amusing mirror of moral admonition laughs at himself during the performance and returns home in a state of mind that evokes self-criticism. . . ."[4] Plavilshchikov stressed the social nature of satire and repeatedly advocated national originality in Russian comedy, insisting particularly on the introduction of real Russian names instead of the conventional "Chestons" and "Erastes."

Krylov lived up to many of these requirements, especially in *The Pie, The Fashion Shop,* and *A Lesson for Daughters* which he wrote at the beginning of the nineteenth century. His own views on playwriting were very similar to Plavilshchikov's. In a review of Klushin's play *Laughter and Sorrow* he wrote: "In the theater the moral lesson ought to be inferred from the action. The playwright ought to show me an envious man whom an orator would describe."[5] This repudiation of didacticism by having the moral lesson inferred from the action and a demand for verisimilitude on the stage was a far cry from the limitations of the Classicist theater. The qualities of Krylov's own plays —their wealth of action, the polish of the characters, and the reduction of the role of the philosophers in the play—become more understandable in the light of his words.

Two aspects of Krylov's comedies must be distinguished: his tribute to the past, which is seen by his traditional plots and limitations to specific character types and secondly, the wish to reflect life realistically. There is but a mere sprinkling of the depiction of everyday life and satire in his comedies. The full development did not come till the fables.

Krylov's battle against the Classicist theater and his political opposition found their fiercest expression in his mock tragedy *Podshchipa* (or, *Trumf*) written in 1800. It was conceived as a literary joke, a high-spirited comedy for the home stage, but eventually outgrew these intentions and developed into a caustic satire on Emperor Paul I and on the autocracy. At the same time it was a brilliant parody on the high style of Classicist tragedy.

This comedy sparkles with merciless irony. Krylov uses venomous sarcasm to ridicule typical Prussian traits which distinguished the Germans who exerted enormous influence in the Russian army during the reign of Paul I. The conqueror, Trumf, however, is not only typical of a dull-witted Prussian martinet who knows only his business of "firing a cannon," but is a caricature of the Russian autocracy and the groveling in front of Prussian and German military by Paul I. Another character in *Podshchipa* is the foolish Tsar Vakul, who amuses himself with a top: "I've played with it since I was a little boy," he says, complaining that a page has broken it. Imbecile courtiers comprise the Tsar's Council, capable only of gorging themselves on a chunk of pork. All this is entertaining farce, portraying the Tsar himself and his ministers in a most unflattering light. Krylov's contemporaries saw this play as a parody on the autocracy. Though it was not published, many copies of it circulated in manuscript form, and it became widely known. The Decembrists, too, understood this mock tragedy as a satirical portrayal of the Russian autocracy. D. Zavalishin commented that "never has a revolutionary written a more malicious satire on the government. Everything and everyone was mercilessly ridiculed, starting from the head of state down to state institutions and private councillors."[6]

Continuing in the tradition of the burlesque parodies of the eighteenth century, such as the mock heroic poems by Vasily I. Maykov, *Podshchipa* parodies the artificial conventions of construction, the far-fetched psychological conflicts, and particularly, the false ring of the lofty style in the pseudo-heroic tragedies.

Krylov's next comedy, *Pirog* (*The Pie*), first staged in 1802, largely keeps to the principles and subject matter of his earlier ones. Its interest lies in the portrayal of daily life and the parody of the oversensitive style of the Sentimentalists who followed in Karamzin's wake. The play has a simple plot based on the opposition of sensible and adroit servants to their frivolous and vain masters. The servants help Preleste, who has been promised in marriage by her parents to a wealthy featherbrain named Fatyuev, to outwit her importunate betrothed and marry her beloved Milon. The play's polemical tendency can best be seen in the satirical portrayal of the quarrelsome Lady Grimace who affects sickly sentimentality. Krylov knows the worth of this sentimentality. The servant, Dasha, describes her mistress in the following words: "... the old woman affects modesty, for her head has been turned by novels and songs; in company she is an angel, but at home nobody is safe from her."[7]

The salient feature of Krylov's plays is his use of realistic comedy and the avoidance of an abstract, moralistic scheme. His comedies were concerned with topical events, and their charac-

ters were prototypes of existing people recognizable to his contemporaries. This lent his plays plausibility, and made the
characters appear not as abstract representations of morals, but
as people with vices and virtues. For example, the worldly and
self-assured Princess Troykin (*The Mischievous Ones*) who
loves to play cards, or Mrs. Chatter, the cynically calculating
and ambitious wife of Rhymestealer in the same play have human
traits which overshadow the conventionality of the contrived
plots and the abstractness of the characters. These early comedies already had the general tendencies and stylistic principles
which come to be fully developed in the Russian Realist comedy
of the nineteenth century.

The upsurge of Russian patriotism during the war against
Napoleon (1805-1807) and at the time of the Peace of Tilsit
(1807), provided him with the subject of his last two comedies,
The Fashion Shop and *A Lesson for Daughters*, written between
1806 and 1807. Their themes go back to his journalistic satire
in *Spirits' Mail* in which he mercilessly ridiculed the Russian
gentry's Gallomania and its disregard of national interests.

The characters of Madame Farre and Monsieur Tricher in *The
Fashion Shop* are similar to the types developed in *Spirits'
Mail*. Other principal characters also have much in common
with Krylov's favorite characters from his earlier comedies;
Muddle, the good-natured provincial landowner reminds one
of Azbukin in *The Mischievous Ones*, and his wife is a recur-
rence of the prototype of the extravagant and vain woman of
fashion.

The Fashion Shop is a much more mature work than his earlier
plays in its reflection of real life, the polish of its characters, the
realism of style, and the fullness and expressiveness of the language. All these features make the honorable Muddle—who
opposes Gallomania—a believable character unlike the boring
philosophizers in eighteenth century comedies. This play has
the embryo of the patriotic theme of Griboedov's famous play
Gore ot uma (*Woe from Wit*).

In 1807 Krylov wrote a one-act comedy, *Lesson for Daughters*,
also ridiculing Gallomania. An amusing vaudeville, the principal characters are provincial ladies who affect the French

style; they dream of French fashions and the pleasures of the capital, and despise their native language. Their father mocks them:

All you know is how to dress or, rather, how to undress, and whether it is more stylish for your hair to fall over your left or your right brow.... But your greatest accomplishment is that you can wag your tongues in French: and as for what you jabber about, God grant that no sane man should ever hear it in any language! (II, 428)

A bankrupt nobleman arrives, and his clever servant—Semyon—deceives these empty-headed ladies by pretending to be a French marquis who has sworn not to talk French. The play is based on the comic effect of misunderstanding, thus anticipating Russian vaudeville of the 1820's and 1840's.

Krylov's fables derived much of their satirical motifs from his plays. The raciness of his fables, the wealth of intonation, and the drama of the plots themselves have also been drawn from his plays. Indeed, his fables have been staged under the title, *Krylov's Fables, A Dramatization.*

III *Journalistic Prose*

Krylov's early works form an integral whole despite the variety of his genres. His comedies, verse, and journalistic satire are all concerned with the injustices of serfdom and the right of the common man to personal happiness. He depicts a whole gallery of tyrannical landowners, willful fops, dissolute, empty-headed noblewomen, predatory money-grubbers, thievish officials, guileful judges, mercenary and incompetent grandees, and in short, all types from all strata of Russian society of his time. Krylov's gift for satire was especially obvious in his journalistic prose and can be compared with the outstanding Russian satirist of the eighteenth century, Nikolay I. Novikov. Possessing great depth of thought and literary merit, this journalistic prose is distinguished by its stinging irony, highly developed scenes of everyday life, and type-casting of its characers, even though he had not yet abandoned the moralistic personification of vice and virtue. His prose was thus closely bound with the Russian

journalistic satire of the 1760's and 1770's which enhanced
Realism in literature. It contained elements of the Realism
which subsequently came to fruition in the works of Gogol and
Saltykov-Shchedrin, and was beginning to overcome the rationalistic abstractness of the Classicists. The urge to give a faithful
portrayal of life greatly affected its style, giving it the sharp
edge of journalistic writing.

The appearance of satirical journals brought literature to a
broader reading public. The heyday of these journals came with
the beginning of the 1760's—a time of social unrest—when public
discontent was rising and finally reached its culmination in the
Pugachev Rebellion. These years saw the appearance of Novikov's *Truten* (*Drone*) and *Zhivopisets* (*Painter*), Fyodor A.
Emin's *Adskaya pochta* (*Hades' Post*), and other lesser journals.
Krylov's satirical journals revived the socially progressive trend
that Novikov had begun, and kept to it even more faithfully.

Pochta dukhov (*Spirits' Mail*) was a one-man journal.[8] It
was not a journal in the modern sense of the word, but a series
of topical satirical writings, a sort of satirical novel. The correspondence of the various "spirits" with the mysterious philosopher,
Malikulmulk, exposed the numerous vices and hypocrisy of high
society, its moral decay, and social injustice. All the letters pur-
sued two themes: the story of the marriage of the worldly fop,
spendthrift, and profligate named Pripryzhkin (Hopskip), and
life in Pluto's underworld and Neptune's underwater kingdoms,
which parody life on earth.

The use of the underworld as a setting for the same kinds of
passions and vices that were prevalent in Russian high society
brought out the absurdity and immorality of their way of life,
and at the same time produced a comic effect. The spirits who
are invisible to men, but themselves can see everything, watch
the mortals' acts from an innocent's point of view; their attitudes are based on the high principles of the Enlightenment,
and man's conduct seems immoral and comic to them. This,
essentially, is Krylov's attitude which tends to be didactic and
moralistic.

Krylov makes extensive use of the favorite device of Enlightenment satire, which can be traced back to Voltaire and

Montesquieu, namely, the description of events from the point of view of the "natural man" whose spirit has not yet been corrupted by "civilization."

A man of the Age of Enlightenment, Krylov believed that ideas ruled the world, that reason and virtue were the corner-stones on which society ought to be founded. The philosophers of the Enlightenment believed that all political and social prob-lems could be solved by legislation and education. Krylov also felt that a moral education based on the philosophy and ethics of the Enlightenment was a necessary prerequisite for attaining a wise and just society. He wrote sharp invectives against injus-tice and the anti-democratic character of tsarist Russia, the back-wardness of its feudal system, and the abuse of power by the ruling classes. The sylph Dalnovid (Far-sighted), one of the cor-respondents in *Spirits' Mail* and the author's mouthpiece, con-cludes his criticism of the aristocracy in the following words:

... the aristocracy will be useful and worthy of respect only when it is attended by virtue; it ought not and cannot ascribe to itself any right to display even one vice: ignorance, folly, dishonesty, and the like, for in the eyes of a philosopher all these foul acts are as repre-hensible in a noble courtier as in the lowest of citizens. (I, 246)

In *Spirits' Mail*, Krylov is relentless in his portrayal of these foul vices not only of the aristocracy, but of officials, judges, and rich peasants and merchants. He draws a picture of the abuse of power and wealth, embezzlement, bribery, corruption, moral decay, and hypocrisy. As a satirist he is not merely a moralist, but an exposer of social evils.

In his protest against the unlimited power of the autocratic monarch, Krylov exposes not only the cruel injustices within the state apparatus, but the corrupting effects of this system on the representatives of power. He presents a gallery of venal self-seekers, brazen-faced oppressors, and slow-witted executors of the despotic regime. He sees the destruction and devastation inflicted on mankind by crowned despots and conquerors, and in the *Spirits' Mail* he echoes the thoughts of the radical French philosopher Louis Sébastien Mercier in an invective against conquerors who slaughter thousands of people and destroy whole states out of vainglory and self-interest. One of the letters reads:

All these imaginary heroes whom blind mortals call by the splendid names of *Great* and *Conqueror* are, in the eyes of a true philosopher, nothing more than Neros and Caligulas; the only difference between them is that the Roman emperors destroyed only people in their own domains, whereas the others massacre citizens of neighboring states, as well as their own. (I, 153)

Krylov produced many historical examples of the harm inflicted by tyrants on their peoples. He particularly condemned despotic rule, aggressive wars, and religious persecutions. He stigmatized conquerors who sacrificed the people for their own inhuman interests:

Ought not a region which has been devastated by a vain conqueror consider him a monster born to destroy the human race? Who gave man the right to kill a million fellow human beings in order to satisfy his foibles? What national law says that many people ought to be sacrificed for the vainglory or, rather, the madness of one man? (I, 153)

One of the most violent attacks on despotism and autocracy is to be found in a letter of the Sylph "Far-sighted," containing a "Discourse on Certain Sovereigns and Ministers" in which he says:

Lions and tigers have inflicted less harm on people than have certain sovereigns and their ministers. Tell me, wisest Malikulmulk, has a lion, driven by fierce hunger, ever hurled himself on another lion like himself and torn him to pieces to satisfy his hunger? Whereas almost every year we see people, who in order to satisfy their vainglory, pride or self-interest, sacrifice human beings like themselves without the slightest pangs of conscience. (I, 153)

This comparison of lions and tigers with sovereigns and their ministers anticipates the use of allegory which Krylov subsequently developed in his fables.

Despite his sympathy for radical and democratic views, Krylov remained a believer in the Enlightenment. This can be seen particularly clearly in his letter "On the Characteristics of Misanthropes" in which he expounds his concept of the state system. In his opinion, the courts of sovereigns ought to include a certain number of misanthropical advisers, at the mere mention of whose name the ministers, judges, and grandees should tremble. Krylov differentiates between misanthropes, such as Timon of Athens, and those who hate not people, but their vices.

This same thought is expressed in the programmatic letter of the Sylph Vysprepar (Airy), which tells of a young sovereign who had only recently ascended the throne. This monarch hears out the precepts of a popular sage who inveighs against court liars and calls on the king to take the people's views into account. Thus, in his youth at least, Krylov's political ideal seems to have been an enlightened monarch who observed the law and acted in the interests of the people. The Enlightenment also influenced Krylov's belief in social equality, one of the tenets of the French Revolution, based on Rousseau's teaching of the natural equality of man.

Krylov opposed the nobility's privileged position and demanded social equality and honest fulfillment of a citizen's duty to the state:

I respect in man only wisdom and virtue. An artisan, a virtuous and honest peasant full of kind-heartedness, is a hundred times dearer to me than a noble who can count as many as thirty titled generations in his family tree, but who has no other merit than the good fortune to have been born to noble parents who, perhaps, brought no more good to their country than did he, but only increased the number of fruitless branches of their family tree. (I, 244)

In his general picture of the morals of court society, Krylov shows their moral decay to be a result of their parisitical mode of life and the loss of patriotic feeling.

Spirits' Mail is not simply a collection of satirical pieces on various subjects. It is an integral work constructed on the principle of Lesage's *Le Diable Boiteux* and Montesquieu's *Lettres Persanes*. For example, the letters of the gnomes named "Sight" and "Tornado" are a satirical attack on contemporary morals—the dissoluteness and hypocrisy of high society—but this unsightly picture is offset by the didactic discourses of the sylphs "Clear-sighted" and "Airy" who criticize the existing state of affairs and preach a morality based on general equality, the good of society, and genuine enlightenment. "Clear-sighted" says:

... casting my glance on the abode of mortals, I am pained to see that the surface of the terrestrial globe inhabited by them is spoiled by a number of people whose existence is totally useless both to themselves and to society, and who not only do not consider it a misfortune to pass as idlers, but by a certain strange bias consider idleness and contempt for the sciences and ignorance as the best arguments for the superiority of man. (I, 79)

This is an expression of the favorite themes of the French Enlightenment, particularly Rousseau's thesis in his *Le Contrat social*, in which he wrote about the baneful influence of idleness and luxury on society.

Illustrating his statements about the dissoluteness of the ruling classes, Krylov presents a whole gallery of libertines and idlers who senselessly and carelessly waste the fruit of their serfs' work. For instance, "Hop-skip" prides himself on squandering money to no purpose and having affairs at every turn. Or his rival, "Waster," whom we meet as he reproaches his faithless mistress:

"Know, inhuman one!" he continues, showing her his right hand decked in signet rings, "know that upon these fingers sits my village of Derelict. My legs are clothed in two villages: Cornless and Plundered. In this expensive watch you see my beloved village of Bledwhite. . . . In short, I can no longer look upon any of my caftans or liveries without being reminded of my mortgaged villages or of a few house serfs that I have sent away as recruits. . . ."

These two styles of narration—the didactic moralizing of the sylphs and the lively satirical portrayal of high society—form a marked contrast which runs throughout the *Spirits' Mail.*

Krylov always shows his characters in social settings, playing their social roles. The grandee, rich peasant, worldly fop, theater courtesan, dissolute coquette, penniless artist, and the court official are all part of a mixed group from various ranks, professions, and classes. Each one of them has his own personal traits of character—or rather moral make-up—determined by his profession and position in society.

Spirits' Mail taught its young author to look at life with vigilance and to understand thoroughly the social nature of human vices and faults. Its characters are endowed with markedly grotesque traits and personify various vices and weaknesses. "Hop-skip" is a spendthrift and fop, a Gallomaniac, and a frivolous squanderer of inherited estates. The frivolous and unvirtuous "Take-me"—whose name describes her well—is a sort of moral tag, which is a very characteristic device of writers of the Enlightenment.

Krylov also satirizes the nobility, court society, and the entire bureaucratic apparatus of Russia in the grotesque description of life in Pluto's underworld kingdom. In this part, he makes use of certain themes from Lucian's *Dialogues of the Gods.* Underworld customs in no way differ from those on earth. Krylov tells that when the dancer Furbiny proves that legs and a respectfully bent back are superior to the head he is appointed first chief of Hades. When Pluto objects, Proserpine cites the example of Emperor Caligula who made his horse a senator: "People now laugh at this, not noticing that the descendants of Caligula's horse have not lost their rank and are spreading all over the world" (I, 228).

Krylov keenly sympathizes with Rousseau's cry against aristocracy and the wealthy, and ruthlessly attacks the social order where wealth and idleness are concentrated at the top of the social ladder, while the lower rungs are occupied by toil and destitution. In *Spirits' Mail* Krylov gives many examples of social inequality and is particularly harsh in denouncing the justice of his time which always inflicted penalties on the poor and justified the rich.

The last letter of the sylph "Far-Sighted," in the second part of *Spirits' Mail,* concludes a moral and social-ethics program and projects the social and moral ideal of the honest man. The very concept of an honest man is equivalent to the concept of a good citizen:

To be completely deserving of the name *honest man* and to merit true praise, one must preserve all the virtues. The lowliest ploughman, if he fulfills this duty of his position with resolution, is more deserving of being called an *honest man* than a proud noble or an incompetent judge. (I, 180)

Krylov's democratic ideal, which he subsequently incorporated in his fables, is combined with a declaration of moral perfection and praise of a simple, working life far from the vanities of the world. Here, too, he expresses the need for moderation and satisfaction with one's lot, a theme which repeatedly appears in his fables. The prosperous man is he who "is happy with his lot and does not envy noble ranks, which are rarely attended by true merit" (I, 181). His views on ethics are sober and practical. He looks for support against the immorality and dissoluteness of high society, counterbalancing it with virtue and the humane principles of the Enlightenment. The moral force of his satire lies in its humanism, typical of Russian social thought and literature. His positive program can be summed up as a demand for an enlightened monarch who would follow the advice of a wise philosopher and protect the interests of the people.

Most of Krylov's articles in *The Observer* and *St. Petersburg Mercury* developed the themes and motifs of *Spirits' Mail*. Worthy of mention is *Pokhvalnaya rech v pamyat moemu dedushke* (*Eulogy in Memory of my Grandfather*), a sharp attack against serfdom in which his gift for satire can be discerned. It can be compared with Novikov's *Letters to Falaley*, Fonvizin's *The Minor*, and to a certain extent, Pushkin's *History of the Village of Goryukhino*. Its accusatory tone, devastating irony, power of expression, and wealth of realistic detail make it one of the best works of Russian satire of the eighteenth century. It describes a typical provincial landowner—an ignorant tyrant, drunkard, and fool—who spends all his time riding to hounds while allowing his serfs to be brought to ruin. There is a convincing description of the landowner's son who is taught from childhood that serfs may be tortured and beaten, but not dogs: "You see, a dog is not a servant: you have to treat it carefully if you do not want to be bitten," lectures the loving father to his worthless son (I, 388). Krylov also attacks the nobility's idyllic conception of Rousseau's ideas: the only book which appeals to the young loafer is Rousseau's *Discourses on the Sciences and Arts*.

With scathing irony Krylov ridicules the nobles who pride themselves on their ancestry: "If it is absolutely necessary that our servants are descended from Adam, we should rather agree to accept the ass as our forefather than be equal to them in descent" (I, 368). This is the same Ass "of noble descent" who subsequently became one of the favorite characters in Krylov's fables.

Krylov imitates with great artistry the eulogy of the slow-witted supporter of serfdom. It is typical that in *The Observer* and *Mercury* he often parodies eulogies (see *Speech of a Rake at a Gathering of Fools* and *Eulogy in Memory of my Grandfather*). This genre—speeches given by negative characters who expose their own poverty of thought—gave Krylov the opportunity of parodying the traditional forms of solemn speeches and sermons, thus creating a lively comic effect. He seems to have been influenced by *In Praise of Folly* by Erasmus, whose realistic satire employs the same literary device of pseudo-panegyric. The importance of this genre is underlined by the fact that Krylov used this type of narration by a simple-minded person later in his fables.

IV *The Tale of* Kaib

Krylov's most successful work of satire is *Kaib: vostochnaya povest* (*Kaib: An Eastern Tale*), published in *The Observer* in 1792. It was singled out by Vissarion Belinsky who pointed out that "it's true merit lies in its satirical mood, sometimes unusually well-aimed and malicious."[9]

It is written in the style of a conventional Eastern allegory, such as that used by Voltaire in his philosophical tales, and reveals the gathering strength of Krylov's talent. A general satirical and philosophical treatise, it is no less ideologically important than the *Spirits' Mail*, but evinces a more mature literary style. Krylov depicts the useless luxury, idleness, and emptiness of court life that he hated so much with a sure and accurate satirical hand.

Kaib satirizes contemporary life and the despotic rule of
Catherine II. The picture of court life which emerges is a
malicious parody of contemporary court customs. For example,
in telling about the position of scholars and writers at the court
of the Caliph, Kaib, Krylov undoubtedly had in mind the
system established by Catherine II: "Although he did not
allow scholars in his court, their pictures were not the least
conspicuous decoration of his walls" (I, 396).

The description of Kaib's divan (council) is a venomous
satire on the autocratic régime. At a meeting, the monarch
announces:

"Gentlemen! I want anyone who objects, to feel free to say so. He
will immediately receive five hundred ox-thong strokes on the soles
of his feet and after that we shall consider his opinion." With this
felicitous introduction Kaib maintained total agreement between himself and the council, and lent his opinions such validity that the
cleverest of the divan wondered at his wisdom. (I, 403)

By making fun of Catherine's liberal phraseology, Krylov gives
a striking example of profound social satire, anticipating the
grotesque style of the nineteenth-century Russian satirist, Saltykov-Shchedrin. The characters of the nobles in Kaib's court are
extremely apt: Dursan (Foolsan), whose importance is measured
by the length of his beard; Oslashid (Assid), who stands out for
his stupidity, but occupies a place in the divan as a birthright;
and cunning Grabiley (Robbiley), who curries favor with
officials and robs the people mercilessly.

Kaib, just as the *Spirits' Mail*, deals with one of the central
political problems of the period—the form that the state system
should adopt. Here, too, Krylov supports the ideal of an enlightened monarchy, and resolutely attacks the despotism and
the arbitrariness of autocratic power. He makes a sharp contrast between sovereigns who are motivated by ambition and
those wise rulers who have concern for the people, defending
the people's interests against autocratic nobles, serf-owning land-
lords, and high officials. The most significant episode dealing
with this problem has Kaib setting out in search of Truth and
meeting the spirit of an ambitious sovereign who delivers a

forceful attack against despotism. Krylov repeats the proposition he has already put forward in *Spirits' Mail*: "Remember," the spirit says to Kaib, "that ambition is punished by excessive humiliation, remember that your power gives you only one right, the right to make people happy" (I, 421).

The fashionable pastoral idyll of Krylov's day is maliciously parodied in the description of Kaib's meeting with a shepherd:

He saw on the river bank a grimy creature, sunburnt and covered with dirt. The Caliph at first doubted that this was a human being, but the bare feet and beard soon convinced him that it was. His appearance was as stupid as his array was poor. "Tell me, my friend," asked the Caliph, "Where is the happy shepherd of this flock?" "That is me," the creature answered and at the same time soaked a stale crust of bread in the stream to make it easier to chew. "You are the shepherd!" Kaib exclaimed in astonishment, "Oh, then you must be able to play the reed pipe beautifully." "That may be, but when I'm hungry I do not feel like playing songs." (I, 417)

Kaib is a consistent and pitiless satire on the autocracy, yet the end of the tale is totally unconvincing: Kaib repents of his past hardheartedness and returns to the throne in order to become a worthy and enlightened ruler. It is possible that this ending was written for the benefit of the censorship, but it is more likely that it expressed the author's general political outlook. Krylov seems to have realized that the ending was unconvincing, for he concludes with the ironic remark that "in our age" such a caliph and his beloved wife "would be considered mad, and people would point their fingers at them" (I, 425).

V Lyric Poetry

The fame of Krylov's fables has overshadowed his poetry. The fact remains, however, that in the 1780's and 1790's, and even later, Krylov had lyric verses, epistles, odes, and epigrams published in various journals. Though his lyric poetry is inferior to his fables, it has its own distinction: Krylov was one of the first poets to develop the genre of "friendly epistles." His epistles are autobiographic in that he expresses his opinions, speaks of his joys and sorrows, and tells about events in his life. He avoids the conventionally abstract manner of Classicist poetry and, instead, writes with true feeling.

In this respect he is close to Derzhavin, and even closer to the homey type of epistle later written by Batyushkov and Pushkin. He speaks of himself as a classless man of plebeian origin, mocking the aristocracy and the hypocrisy and dissoluteness of its worldly entourage. In a friendly epistle to Klushin he describes his ideal of an independent and honest man in the autobiographical character of the subject of the poem:

> I've always hated fuss and trouble,
> In summer lounged in winter coat;
> I've never striven for splendid ranks
> Nor deemed it happiness and bliss
> To feel contempt for common man.
> I have not paused at great men's halls;
> I've taken pride in one rank only,
> And that I bear by nature's law:
> The rank of man; to possess that
> Has been a duty and a joy.
> To be a man, no more, no less
> Is genuine glory, the only pride.   (II, 222)

To respect this "rank of man," that is, to be a human being and a true citizen was young Krylov's motto. His declaration of the superiority of "the rank of man" over the rank of noble, and his protests against class and social inequality likened him to Radishchev. Krylov emphasized in his poetry that he held "honesty higher than gold" and did not equate "conscience and wealth."

Noteworthy among Krylov's lyric verses are the epistles, satires, and epigrams in which he developed the lightness and skill that prepared him for the poetical technique of his fables.

CHAPTER 3

The People's "Book of Wisdom"

I Turning to the Fable

ALL of Krylov's previous literary work was a preparation for writing fables. His experience in writing for *Spirits' Mail* brought political topicality and satire to his fables. The theatrical effect and comical portrayal of the characters in his plays helped him create the miniature scenes of his fables and enliven them with playful humor. And, finally, his experience in writing lyric poetry taught him how to handle verse with expertise. When his first book of fables appeared in 1809—eighteen fables which had been printed in journals from 1806—it was immediately evident that Krylov was a complete master of the art. Krylov spent almost thirty years in adding to this collection. The last edition, which he compiled shortly before his death and which appeared in print in December 1843, contained 197 fables.

Krylov wrote his fables sparingly—only a few each year— and worked on each one with great thoroughness. "I read my new verses until some of them do not seem to belong to me, that is, I get to dislike them. Then I correct them or change them altogether."[1]

In his fables Krylov expounded the views of the Enlightenment which he had adopted as a young journalist. He started writing fables at a period when the predominant trend in Russian literature was Sentimentalism, and Romanticism was just emerging. The tone for poetry was set by Karamzin, Zhukovsky, Dmitriev, Vasily L. Pushkin (uncle of A. S. Pushkin), and the young Batyushkov. The maudlin sentimentality of Karamzin's followers found expression in the emotional lyricism of their poetry in which they tried to attain intimacy and a lightness of touch. These characteristics also appeared in the fables. Dmitriev's, Zhukovsky's, and Vasily Pushkin's fables had an intimate, oversensitive character. They provided a contrast to the coarseness and satirical harshness of Sumarokov's fables by representing mostly elegant scenes from gentry life. Their greatest merit was considered to be the elegance of the narrative itself. The journal *Tsvetnik* (Flower Bed), for example, published a rapturous review of a fable by Dmitriev, which said: "The main gift of a fabulist is the ability to tell a story well, and Mr. Dmitriev is magnificently endowed with this gift.... He combines a profound knowledge of the language with simplicity and a good-natured wit which seems to come all of its own, flowing spontaneously."[2]

Fables written in the style of Sentimental poetry were off home ground and lost their satirical tendency; they were turned into a salon genre—witty epigrams.

Such was the literary climate when Krylov published his first fables. He refused to subordinate the fable to the requirements of salon elegance in the manner of the Sentimentalists, and restored its popular sources and satirical tendencies. This was not, however, a return to the traditions of the Sumarokov school. Krylov rejected the coarseness and Naturalistic burlesque of Sumarokov's fables and reached a high level of perfection in the art of fable writing. His fables heralded the birth of Realism and were also closely linked with folklore. They were an important literary event, introducing a new, democratic understanding of life and new artistic principles opposed to the esthetics of the Sentimentalists.

II *National Character*

Krylov explained that he turned to writing fables because "this style is comprehensible to everybody; servants and children read them."[3] This meant simply that Russian literature was no longer the exclusive property of the salons of the nobility; it was now to be part of real life.

The fables of Sumarokov and subsequently, Krylov, were widely read by the people in illustrated, cheap, popular editions. The national character and democratic tendencies of Krylov's fables were prized even by his contemporaries. Thus, in 1825 Alexander Pushkin wrote about Krylov and La Fontaine:

They will both remain beloved by their compatriots. It has been justly remarked that artlessness (*naïveté, bonhomie*) is an innate trait of the French people; our characteristic feature is a certain playfulness, a mocking, colorful way of expressing ourselves: La Fontaine and Krylov represent the spirit of their nations.[4]

On another occasion Pushkin called Krylov the most popular Russian poet.

Gogol valued the national character of Krylov's fables no less than Pushkin. In his article, *What in Fact is the Essence of Russian Poetry and What Are Its Peculiar Features?* (1842) he wrote: "It would be a grave mistake to consider [Krylov] a fabulist in the same sense as La Fontaine, Dmitriev, Khemnitser or Izmaylov. His parables are the property of the people and make up a book of the wisdom of the people themselves."[5]

Both Pushkin and Gogol perceived the importance of Krylov's fables for their blending of the national and popular character with a spirit of democracy. Krylov's popular character (*narodnost'*) is not only deeply national, but is untainted by any kind of stylization. It arises naturally because of the author's grasp of the people's speech and their attitude toward life. For this reason, Pushkin and Gogol saw in Krylov something of a standard of *narodnost'* and national character. Belinsky qualified this definition by pointing to certain limitations of this *narodnost'* within the frame of the fable. He considered Krylov a poet of the people by nature, but indicated: "Pushkin's poetry reflected all of Russia, with all its essential elements and all the different sides to its national soul. Krylov expressed, albeit widely and fully, only one side of the Russian soul—its common, practical sense, its worldly wisdom, its simple-heartedness, and bitter irony."[6]

This qualification is justified: the limitations imposed by the fabulist's genre prevented Krylov from embracing every aspect of life. But Belinsky is not justified in claiming that Krylov's fables depict only the "common, practical sense," for they also give a broad social picture of life in Russia at the beginning of the nineteenth century.

The greater part of Krylov's fables were written in the first third of the nineteenth century, a time when Russian social thought was being developed by the nobility and when the most famous writers were those who depicted life from the nobility's point of view. Krylov's popular wisdom was not confined to the peasant's way of thinking which was often conservative; it also included positive features characteristic of the people as a whole: traits of national character and the democratic sentiments of the working masses. Krylov's political views were, however, often limited and he hoped that the people's lot could be improved by the leaders. He was under the illusion that society could be perfected through enlightenment and education.

His fables depict the customs and social vices of Russian life in serf-owning Russia. The very fact that Krylov censured social inequality by dividing his characters into rich and famous ones who do nothing but harm to the people, and honest, hard workers, is a sign of his democratic inclinations. Felt throughout the fables is Krylov's ironic and hostile attitude to the titled ruling circles with their selfishness, presumption, greed, idleness, and pompous stupidity. His fables show ministers, nobles, the tsar himself, and officials of all ranks as being cruel, selfish, treacherous, and hypocritical oppressors of the people, concerned solely with their own welfare. He judges them from the point of view of the toiling masses who despise these privileged parasites, and he represents them by predatory lions, wolves, and bears. Krylov's fables have one thing in common: the contrast between the rulers and the common man. The people represent the good qualities—genuine humanity, patriotism, love of freedom, a strong moral sense, and industry. They are contrasted to despotic nobles, self-interested officials, the rapacious and cynical wealthy class, and corrupt representatives of the privileged classes.

III *Patriotism*

Krylov affirmed the patriotic sentiments of the people and the progressive intelligentsia. This is apparent in his understanding of the popular character of the Patriotic War of 1812, displayed in the fables he wrote in that period. In *Crow and*

Fowl, Wolf in the Kennels, and *A Train of Carts* he gives a high appraisal of Marshal Kutuzov's activity as a popular general and showed that it was his farsighted strategic plan that had led to the victory over Napoleon. *Wolf in the Kennels* expresses the urge of the Russian people to drive the foreign aggressors out of the country and shows the upsurge of patriotic sentiments. *Crow and Fowl* is a biting attack on the contemptible turncoat crows who are devoid of patriotic feeling and who think they can get along with "the guests" who have come to conquer them. In *Sharing Up* Krylov censures the selfishness and indifference of the ruling circles to the common cause of defending their country, an indifference shown at a time of national patriotic fervor evoked by Napoleon's invasion. He likens them to "partners in trade" who argue about the division of profits while the whole house is on fire. Krylov contrasts the people's readiness to face misfortune and sacrifice to those concerned only about their profits:

> And in affairs far greater, that I know,
> I've seen how all concerned have gone to ruin so;
> By way of joining hands to meet the common blow,
> Each starts some wrangle of his own
> For self and self alone. (II, 6)°

Wolf in the Kennels, Crow and Fowl, A Train of Carts, and *Sharing Up* were written at the height of the war. In his censure of the faint-hearted (*Crow and Fowl*) and in his call for unity to defeat the foe (*Sharing Up*) and drive him out of the country (*Wolf in the Kennels*), Krylov was voicing the sentiments of the Russian people. These fables differ from his others: they are noted not so much for their irony and humor as for their patriotism.

Wolf in the Kennels is a highly dramatic work. It expresses the tragedy of the people during the worst period of the war and reveals Napoleon's difficult position after the Battle of Borodino in the face of the Russian people's will to win. Napoleon actually

---

° All fables included herein, with one exception, were translated by Bernard Pares. *See:* Bibliographical entry. *Fishes Dancing* was translated by the author.

sent a French ambassador, Loriston, to Kutuzov with an offer
of peace, but Kutuzov rejected it. This historical fact was used
to symbolize the Russian people's unshakable will to defeat the
enemy. The very first lines of the fable are strikingly epic in
scope; they convey the Russian people's vigilance and readiness
to repulse the enemy and perform selfless martial deeds:

> A wolf that came to scale the fold by night,
> > Did on the kennels light;
> The kennels, straight, are live as day;
> The hounds, that scent so near their old grey enemy,
> Throng at the kennel doors and press to meet the fray.
> > "Ho, boys, a thief! a thief!" the keepers cry;
> The court-yard gates swing back; the bolts that instant fly;
> > The place is hot as hell next minute.
> > > With doughty club comes one,
> > > The next with gun.
> "Bring lights," they cry, "bring lights"; and some for torches run.

This is a picture of the national patriotic upsurge which united
all the best people in Russia. And opposed to it is the Wolf
(Napoleon), the perfidious enemy, who finds himself in a trap,
not having counted on meeting with a national rebuff. This
wolf is not so much pitiful as evil and cunning. The energetic
tone at the beginning changes to a slow and detailed description:

> Wolf at the corner sits, his stiff grey back well in it;
> He shows his snarling teeth, he bristles up his hair;
> He looks as if his eyes would eat them then and there;
> > But as with dogs it's folly to begin it,
> > And after all, it's certain quite,
> > > There's no free mutton for to-night,
> > > Our sly old wolf thinks right
> > > > To try a parley.   (II, 8)

His teeth are chattering, his fur is bristling, and he is obliged
to ask for an amicable arrangement; gone are all thoughts of
fighting, his main concern now is to save his skin. He adopts
a humble, though at the same time familiar tone, wishing to
imitate the manner of the dogs surrounding him ("My friends,
why all this pother?" he says.)

This unattractive figure, obliged to lie and fawn to preserve his life is contrasted to the Head-Keeper who has the wisdom and dignity of a peasant. He is not so much a portrait of Kutuzov as a monumental picture of the Russian people. This is why his words sound like a wise popular verdict:

> My hair is white, if yours is grey.
> For my idea of wolves I long have had my grounds;
> And this, the plan I've always tried;
> I count no truce with wolf is ratified
> Before I've stripped him of his hide! (II, 8)

This speech is made in the name of the people, and its irreconcilable tone gave the Russian people faith and courage in the days of their severest stress. One can understand why this fable was so popular with the Russian army during the War of 1812. According to contemporaries: "Krylov personally copied the fable and gave it to Kutuzov's wife who sent it in a letter to her husband. Kutuzov read it after the battle by the town of Krasny to a gathering of officers and men, and when he came to the words 'My hair is white' he took off his white cap and shook his bowed head."

IV Moral Ideal

The accusatory themes of Krylov's fables give an idea of his moral outlook on life. It is based on a morality that adopts virtues inherent to the working man. This is fully expressed in the fable *Leaves and Roots* which affirms that the basis of existence is in the work of the people. The bragging of the idle leaves and tree crown whose shade and beauty entice shepherdesses to dance under them is contrasted to the mighty roots which feed the tree with life-giving juices, so that the branches and leaves can give this shade:

> The roots of that same tree on which yourselves you grow.
> Then flaunt, the summer through;
> And yet this difference between us, keep in view!
> When spring returns again, new leaves wave hither, thither,
> But if but once the roots should wither,
> The tree is gone, and so are you. (IV, 2)

The roots are the people who are the life force of the country. Krylov ridicules parasites on the basis of a moral code of the people, thus displaying his awareness of the lofty mission of a citizen and writer. Arising from behind the mockery and exposure of hypocrisy and lawlessness is the ideal of the Enlightenment: a demand for democratic equality, and faith in justice, law, and the curative effects of rational principles on society.

This ideal is embodied in the bee, the traditional symbol of toil. In his foreword to *Eagle and Bee* Krylov expresses his opinion of the social system:

'Tis well with him whose part in public must be played.
    All through it keeps his spirit warm
To know the world will watch the deeds he must perform;
Yet honour also him down yonder in the shade,
Whose unrewarded toil through long and weary days
        Can win no glory and attract no praise:
            One only thought to cheer his labour:—
            His work will benefit his neighbour.   (II, 14)

"Common good" is part of the terminology of the Enlightenment, but Krylov gives it a specifically democratic meaning, likening the bearers of this "good" to the diligent and selfless bees. Moreover, he counterposes the eagle, "on every side scattering dread" and bringing confusion and harm, to the vital work of the unassuming bee. Krylov also adopted the point of view of the working man in assessing both the vices of the society around him and the good qualities of man. *Old Mat and his Man* is also democratic in spirit; it is an account of the magnanimity and heroism of the poor peasant and the self-seeking and ingratitude of the rich peasant. Its social implications are far broader than the event it describes: a bear attacks a peasant and crushes him under his weight; it seems that the old man has no hope of survival, but a farm laborer who happens to be nearby does not lose his nerve and

He swings his axe, and smites off half the skull,
Then drives his pitch-fork home clean through the creature's paunch;
    Bear roars, and tumbles to the ground half-dead.
        While there he breathes his last,

Old Matthew, now the danger's past,
Heaps curses on his saviour's head.
Poor Steve stands rooted to the spot;
"Here, come! What's that for, Mat?" "You dolt, you ask for what?
For God's sake drop that foolish grin!
Your clumsy axe has spoilt the skin!"   (II, 19)

The main theme of this fable is human ingratitude, but the old peasant's greed and ingratitude are not simply a human fault—they are a trait of the rich proprietor.

Apart from being a satirist, Krylov was also a moralist, sharing the conviction of the Enlightenment that sermons and satire could improve the ways of society. Some of his sermons, however, are lifeless and devoid of realistic color and the fable degenerates into a didactic discourse. This was most often the case when he tried to prove his loyalty. The resulting fables are unsuccessful from a literary point of view (*The Godless Tribe, The Pearl Divers, Horse and Rider,* and *Author and Robber*). Where, however, Krylov expresses the people's point of view, his moralizing takes on a living force and becomes a true picture of real life. The common people are shown in all their diversity. Their deep-seated faults and contradictions in human relationships are described with playful humor and Krylov affirms the robust egalitarian morality inherent in the people's thinking. For example, *The Peasant in Distress* is devoted to selfish indifference to another's misfortune: A peasant's entire house is burglarized, but instead of giving him practical help, his friends offer him hypocritical condolences and advice, which —though fair enough in their own right—do not lighten the destitute peasant's load.

"My poor, my worthy friend"—Old Thompson makes a speech—
"What need had you to boast for all the town to hear,
        Your riches were so great!"
Then cousin Bill cuts in: "Ah, well, in future, mate,
You'll sharpen up your wits, and build your store-room near."   (III, 2)

The fable reveals a detailed knowledge of peasant life and is full of biting irony against such "know-it-alls" who are only too pleased to give advice. It does not occur to them—or rather,

they have no wish—to offer real help to their friend. The irony
is made much more malicious when Foka (Noggs) offers the
unfortunate peasant one of his bitch's puppies for the only
reason that it does not cost him anything:

> "You come to me, and choose you out a pup!
> 'Tis one of Fan's you know; I'm glad to give it up—
> To help a friend, why not?
> I'd only drown the lot!"   (III, 2)

Krylov's intimate knowledge of peasant life enabled him
to produce fables which were not about idyllic shepherds, but
about real peasants, with their weaknesses and virtues, neither
embellished nor burlesqued, as were Sumarokov's peasants. In
the fable *Two Countrymen,* for example, peasant life is depicted
accurately, though sparingly; their troubles are seen through
their own eyes. Krylov avoided any sort of allegory; the characters are simple peasants who have become cripples as a result
of their excessive love of wine. They tell each other the story
of their mutilation: Faddey (Tom) burned his courtyard to
ashes when he set off with a candle to feed his horses at
Christmas with his head singing from the merrymaking. Yegor
(Will) wanted to avoid causing a fire on just such an occasion
and went down into the cellar without a candle. He fell off the
ladder and was crippled. Krylov turns these everyday incidents
into significant events. The accuracy with which he portrays
such situations is what makes his fables so graphic.

The code of morals presented in Krylov's fables assesses a
man's conduct in relation to specific situations and to the good
they may bring society. Fables such as *Cat and Cook, Gardener
and Wiseacre,* and *The Miller* advocate a positive attitude to
life, as opposed to passive contemplation and inactivity. Krylov's morality springs from the common sense of the people
themselves, and he ridicules parasites, idlers, and fools as for
instance, his Trishka (Sammy) who fashions a new coat out
of an old one (*Sammy's Coat,* IV, 8), the happy-go-lucky lazy
Miller through whose dam "the water worked its way," or the
awkward, "industrious" bear who in vain shattered enormous
quantities of birch, walnut, and elm.

At the same time that he exposes the injustices of the social order in which the weak are oppressed by the strong and sharply criticizes despotism, extortion by the authorities, and the hypocrisy of he Tsar himself, Krylov advances his ideal of the honest and noble patriot who works for the common good. For him, the greatest virtue and main duty of the citizen is to serve his country. In *Bee and Flies* he says:

> Who tries to serve his country rightly,
>   Will never leave her lightly.
> The idler who can serve no public use
> May well on foreign soil his greatest pleasure find; (VI, 13)

Yet, for all his criticism of the feudal system Krylov did not draw the logical revolutionary conclusions. In his fables, *Horse and Rider, Author and Robber, A Blade of Corn,* and *The Godless Tribe,* he remained a moralist of the Enlightenment and censured revolutionary change. Especially was he very much against the French Revolution. His limited thinking was also apparent in his belief that social contradictions could be reconciled. In *A Blade of Corn* he calls on working people to reconcile themselves to their subordinate position and advises the blades which grow under difficult conditions of intense heat and bad weather not to envy the lot of greenhouse flowers. The fable ends in a sermon calling on everyone to reconcile himself to his lot and not to grumble about it.

His ideas, influenced by the Enlightenment, were no abstract philosophy, but were closely bound with real life. His fables deal not only with moral principles, but with specific rules of conduct for everyday life. They preached kindness, honesty, and justice, ridiculing human weaknesses such as greed, boastfulness, impudence, lying, lack of conscientiousness, and incompetence. His Monkeys, Asses, Foxes, Elephants, Wolves, and Bears represent negative characters and their animal nature graphically brings out their faults.

And while he valued work and talent, he valued modesty no less.

> Who prates of his affairs incessantly to all,
>   In him, be sure, the worth is small.

> The man of action oftenest speaks low;
> 'Tis by their sounding deeds the great their greatness show,
> But turn their weighty projects round
> Without a sound.   (VI, 5)

Thus ends the fable *Two Casks*, about an empty cask that thunders down the road, and a full one of wine which completes its journey in silence. The main theme running through all his work is that of a man's civic duty, the good he brings society, and his devotion to his people and country.

Fables have retained their popular essence throughout their centuries of existence, and have always been an expression of the people's thoughts. This is why the numerous salon fables of the eighteenth and nineteenth centuries have been forgotten while Krylov's fables have retained not only their literary impact, but the force of the people's verdict. Krylov's fables grew out of the wisdom of Russian sayings and proverbs with their keen humor.

Belinsky wrote about Krylov: "A popular poet . . . always rests on a firm basis—the nature of his people."[7]

V *National Form*

What constitutes the originality of Krylov's fables? He makes use of traditional animal characters to represent human failings and endows them with extraordinarily lifelike traits, reproducing typical aspects of contemporary Russian life. Despite limitations imposed by the conventions of fable writing upon the realistic portrayal of life and the necessity for didacticism, Krylov managed to create lively pictures of typical Russian life. His characters, including the animals, are not abstract allegories, but living people with their own particular character.

Gogol remarked that "apart from his ability to depict animals—at which he is so good that not only the fox, the bear, and the wolf, but even the earthenware pot seems to be alive—they contain the very spirit of the Russian countryside. . . . In short, his works live and breathe Russia."[8]

This is in essence what Belinsky said, too:

Someone once said that the bear in Krylov's fables is a Russian bear and the hen—a Russian hen; everyone laughed at these words, but they are based on good sense, comic though they sound. The point is that Krylov's best fables are not about bears or foxes, although on the surface it would seem that they are the subject of the action, but about people, and what is more, about Russian people.[9]

In *The Soup of Master John* (Demyan's Fish Soup) both Demyan (John) and his unfortunate neighbor Foka (Tom) are typical Russians: One is an obstinate, hospitable buffoon, and the other a staid, conventional fellow. The entire scene is played out in a peasant's cottage which is typically Russian, both because Russian characters are shown and because of the graphic rendering of the atmosphere through the peasants' way of life. In addition, Demyan's and Foka's language is the rich and expressive language of the people, natural and untainted by vulgar burlesque.

Krylov's fables lose none of their originality or national character despite the fact that many of the plots are borrowed from La Fontaine. Or, as Belinsky wrote: "Even though he took the content of some of his fables from La Fontaine, he cannot be called a translator: his exceptionally Russian character breathed Russian life into everything he touched."[10] Krylov would take a traditional fable plot and not only Russify the context, but often even substitute his own moral for the original one, to fit in with his views. His first fables, *Oak and Reed, The Dainty Spinster,* and *The Old Man and Three Young Dandies,* were based on La Fontaine's plots, but were not translations; they were, rather, national equivalents.

The Dainty Spinster was based on La Fontaine's *La Fille,* but its background is typically Russian: The lady is sent suitors by matchmakers in accordance with the Russian custom and the suitors "drive daily to her door to pay her court." What could be more Russian! The bride herself is given traits typical of a noble girl from a fairly well-to-do family. In La Fontaine, on the other hand, "la belle les trouva trop chétifs de moitié." When the bride develops into an old maid, Krylov characterizes the situation with the following touch: "But now, alas! alas! it's 'don't you play at cards?'" while in La Fontaine there is no such detail nor could there have been.

The originality of a fable lies not in its plot, but in the

author's telling of it. The interpretation of the plot and the colorfulness of the narrator's language are what have allowed different fabulists to turn to the same plots century after century.

Mistress and Her Two Maids is another example of a fable the plot of which is borrowed from La Fontaine's fable of the same name, but which is nonetheless an episode from Russian life. The maids have become Russian girls, exhausted by their tireless old mistress who makes them rise with the crowing of the cock and forces them to work long hours at spinning. The old woman with her "cloak of fur" and "widow's cap," and the girls, sitting at the spindle on weekdays and holidays, all smack of Russia.

Plots already made famous by La Fontaine acquired a Russian color in Krylov's hands. He altered details, added new ones, lengthened or shortened the story (more often shortened, as conciseness was one of his characteristics). The main point is, however, that his fables are much more realistic and satirical than La Fontaine's.[11] Furthermore, Krylov is totally free of La Fontaine's Classical conventions and somewhat dry reserve.

Krylov delighted in describing conditions of everyday life. He did not shrink from hinting at topical events and poking fun at them. From Classicism he drew merely the form and discipline of the composition, and the precision of poetical vision and expression. The realistic manner of execution, the wealth of satirical tones, the more evident kinship with popular humor, and the extensive use of national folk traditions, all contributed to making his fables realistic.

Krylov did not change La Fontaine's plots merely by contributing natural color to their telling. His most important distinctive trait is in the "merry playfulness" and "mockery and colorful way of expressing himself" as Pushkin mentioned in his review when he compared him with La Fontaine. "Playfulness," verbal "colorfulness," and the ability to spot and convey human weaknesses or the negative side of social phenomena are distinguishing features of Russian popular satire of the seventeenth century, and Krylov's fables inherited the malicious rough humor of those works. In those early popular satires, such as *Tale of Mr. Hedgehog* and *The Trial of Shemyaka*, one can already feel the expressiveness of Russian popular speech, and the people's hate and contempt for judges, officials, and all those who helped to oppress the people, using their positions to increase their personal wealth.

In taking over La Fontaine's plots, Krylov created virtually a new fable, usually by setting it in a background of Russian manners and morals. Sometimes even the countryside becomes typically Russian as in *Gadfly and Ant*: Now the fields lie bleak and dead,/ All those days of sunshine fled . . . (II, 12).

Spendthrift and Swallow, taken from Aesop, has an accurate description of a Russian winter, which, it goes without saying, was not even hinted at in Aesop:

> And so it proves! The frosts return again;
> The carts go creaking through the crumbled snow;
> The chimneys puff their smoke; on every window pane
> Delightful fairy tracings show.   (VII, 4)

When Krylov took La Fontaine's plot for *The Peasant and Death*, his subject was the difficult life of the peasant in feudal Russia and not somewhere else:

> His faggots on his back, in winter's bitterest cold,
> Worn out with toil and stress, a peasant frail and old,
> With heavy sighs and groans, each moment faltering more,
> Towards his smoky hut his heavy burden bore . . .
>   "Lord, what a wretched man am I!
> Kept short of everything, with wife and children too;
> Ground rent and master's dues, and tax on tax to pay." (V, 10)

Writing about Krylov's fables, Belinsky commented that "he fully exhausted and expressed . . . a whole aspect of the Russian character: the Russian practical sense is reflected in his fables as in a polished mirror. . . . They contain all the worldly wisdom, the fruit of practical experience, both his own and that handed down from father to son"[12]

VI *Folk Sources*

In depicting reality Krylov strove to develop criteria which would reflect the attitudes of the people. He continually turned to proverbs, which is why his style is very reminiscent of them. Many of his fables illustrate proverbs, draw similar morals, and have a similar understanding of reality. The use of proverbs and sayings lend his fables national color and flavor. Proverbs provided him with colorful and laconic formulas for expressing his own views and the honest and satirical attitude of the people to the negative aspects of life. He made use of characters from proverbs and folk tales, and, with striking artistic perfection, combined the caustic popular humor of the proverb with its powers of verbal expression and apt evaluation of contemporary reality. In the course of this process, he enriched the popular characters of the proverbs.

In these proverbs, Krylov found satirical formulas of extreme precision and conciseness for characterizing the most varied aspects of contemporary life, as well as a moral evaluation of the behavior of man. Proverbs are the most graphic expression of Russian popular humor, understanding of life, moral sense, and repudiation of unjust social customs. They achieve the utmost expressiveness and universality of application while remaining figurative.

Many of Krylov's fables have their very origin in proverbs. For example, the proverb: "Don't spit in the well, it'll come in useful for drinking water" determines the plot and moral of *Lion and Mouse. Poor Rich Man* and *The Miser* are closely connected with proverbs about miserliness. In many cases proverbs determine not only the moral, but also the plot of a fable, turning it into an expanded metaphor. Such, for example, is *Tom-Tit.* The proverb is: "Tom-Tit flew towards the sea, to set it all on fire; it raised a din with rowdy glee, but nothing came of all its ire." Krylov's fable is, in a manner of speaking, a development of this proverb. It relates how the tomtit boasted that it wanted to burn the sea, and how it raised a fearful din in its boasting:

> In Neptune's capital° the frightened dwellers swarm;
>   The birds in squadrons form;
> The beasts of all the woods come streaming in to see,
> How well the sea will burn, and what the heat will be. (I, 15)

° Neptune's capital: Petersburg.

He dwells at great length on the effect created by the bird's bragging; and this is a pretext for introducing a series of scenes from real life, showing typical traits of official society and relating the fable not to the conventional mythological situation, but to the metropolitan manners and morals of St. Petersburg.

Proverbs were not merely a source for many of Krylov's fables, but determined the structural principle which potentially holds the plot of a fable. Popular proverbs also taught Krylov to be sparing with words and thus make short, memorable formulas of his fables. This explains why entire lines and many expressions from his fables have, in their turn, become proverbial.

All the same, the fundamental difference between a proverb and a fable must not be overlooked. The proverb provides the bare meaning, while the fable gives the flesh and blood of poetic images. It is the telling of the fable that determines the fabulist's poetical individuality. This connection with popular sources and the creative genius of the people themselves are the reasons for the unfading vitality and freshness of Krylov's fables. The ironic presentation of the animals links them organically with the folk tale. The cunning, gossipy fox, the greedy wolf, the stupid bear, and others have been borrowed from folk tales.

The fable *Fox* has even taken its plot from the well-known tale about the Wolf and the Fox. It relates how the Fox's tail froze stiff in an ice-hole, or rather, how the fur on the tip of his tail froze, but the Fox was loath to lose it and waited till the whole tail had frozen. He was then forced to ask for the Wolf's help, and the Wolf, of course, gnawed the Fox's tail all the way off. The affinity to the folk tale is not confined to the plot, for its very flavor and poetical color shows us the Russian folk tale with its special poetry and humor. The Fox's tail, for example, is described thus: "a tail so soft and downy, So fluffy and so ruddy-browny." The playful humor of the moral has a very folk-tale-like ring about it: "To see this fable's point, I think you will not fail./ A hair just here or there the fox need not bewail,/ If only he can keep his tail!" (IX, 4).

Many of the other fables are also told in the manner of folk tales. Their very first lines set the tone of an oral tale: "One day the mice conspired to make the world ecstatic" (*Mice in Coun-*

cil), "Now once there was an ant whose strength was quite enormous" (*The Strong Ant*).

Krylov played a decisive role in making Russian literature truly national. Belinsky wrote that "Ivan Andreevich Krylov is the nearest Russia has to a national poet; he will become one as soon as the Russian people become literate. Moreover, he will pave the way for other poets' *narodnost'* in literature."[13] Belinsky's prediction has been totally justified. Krylov did in fact pave the way to *narodnost'* (spirit of the people) for Pushkin, Koltsov, and Nekrasov in literature.

Belinsky by no means equated the popular character of poetry with mere derivation from folklore; he understood it as the extent to which the spirit of a nation was expressed. That is why he saw an "enormous difference" between the popular character of Krylov's poetry and that of Pushkin.

Belinsky's critiques are crucial to the understanding of Krylov. They determine the character of Krylov's popularity and the extent of his national significance, which is different in every writer; and they explain why it was Krylov and not some other writer who opened the way for other poets to become popular writers.

CHAPTER 4

Satire

I *Aesopic Language*

IN his satirical picture of the upper classes and contemporary
morals, Krylov sharply attacked the Russian serf-owning
society.

After the war against Napoleon had been won by the people,
tsarism exploited the victory and charted a reactionary course.
However, simultaneously with the introduction of police meas-
ures for safeguarding the serf system, Alexander I often resorted
to a false liberalism to pacify growing discontent on the part of
the people.

The intensification of reactionary and arbitrary rule was especially evident when Alexander entrusted the government to
his cruel and incompetent favorite, General Alexis Arakcheev.
The best of the nobility joined the secret Decembrist movement
to protest the autocratic police regime and popular discontent
increased.

Such was the situation when Krylov wrote his fables. Although
he did not agree with the Decembrists, he continually criticized
the regime, and allegory enabled him to write what he thought,
something he would not have been able to do in a direct manner.
Whereas the ancient fables of Aesop and Phaedrus, and the fables
of the eighteenth century were, on the whole, moral sermons,
Krylov's fables were satires of pressing topicality.

In the nineteenth century Belinsky was already saying that

today, the fable as a moralizing form of poetry is not a genuine
form. . . . But as satire, it is a genuine form of poetry . . . Aesop is
irrelevant to our times. There is nothing difficult about thinking up
a subject for a fable; in fact, one does not need to invent one: one
can pick it ready-made, but one must be able to *tell* and *adapt* it.

75

The telling and the moral constitute the essence of the fable; satire and irony are its most important qualities.[1]

Krylov's satire is full of broad generalizations. Its target is not merely human weaknesses and failings, but, to an even greater extent, the injustice of the social system which gave rise to them. The incompatibility between wealth and poverty, social status and the innate qualities of man, the hierarchy of officials and the oppression of the people were all problems with which Krylov was concerned.

Krylov wrote his fables in a series of hints and allegories commonly called Aesopic language. Krylov himself called it: "saying the truth half-openly." This manner of writing was later brilliantly developed by the great Russian satirist Saltykov-Shchedrin. In Aesopic language Krylov was able not only to write about matters not allowed by the censorship, but to create a "system" of ironic hints and pointed comic situations. The reader knew very well that the various animals in the fables were not fictional beasts, but represented real people, whether types or actual historical personages, living or dead. The important point is that the satirical application of the fable was broadened by Krylov, so that it is much more general than some minor event which may have prompted its writing originally. This is, of course, what makes Krylov's fables as interesting and relevant today as they were when he wrote them.

II   *Political Opposition*

The plots and characters of fables are so traditional that fabulists have almost acquired the right to express themselves freely and unhampered by the censorship. This is not only because of the Aesopic language used in fables, but also because the characters are so popular and well-known, and have such generally applicable traits that it is impossible to connect them with any particular fact or person even when the author intends a connection to be made. Indeed, this is why—despite his critical attitude in his satire—Krylov was never persecuted, but was even patronized by the tsarist authorities. Only two or three of his fables were not passed by the censorship. The fables were written in such an objective and popular style that it would have been as difficult to ban them as it would be to ban proverbs.

Alexander Herzen appreciated Krylov's critical attitude for its importance in the development of progressive social thought: "Before Nicholas I's accession to the throne, opposition literature had something reticent and conciliatory about it; its mockery was not altogether bitter. We find this in the astonishing fables of Krylov (their oppositional significance has never been properly appreciated)."[2] Herzen placed Krylov's fables on a par with Griboedov's *Woe from Wit,* although at the same time he pointed to the lack of consistency and the reticent nature of this opposition.

The Decembrists saw in Krylov's fables themes and ideas close to their heart, and held him in high esteem. In a survey of Russian literature published in *Polyarnaya zvezda* (*The Polar Star—* the Decembrist almanac) for 1823, Alexander Bestuzhev (Marlinsky) wrote:

I. Krylov raised the Russian fable to a level of original Classicism. It would be impossible to narrate with more simplicity, in a more popular language or with a more palpable moral. Every one of his verses reveals Russian practical sense. His descriptions of nature resemble those of La Fontaine, but retain their special character; each one of his fables is satire and draws strength from the fact that it is short and is told with an air of simplicity.[3]

(Bestuzhev thus anticipated Belinsky in stressing the satirical inclinations of Krylov's fables.)

One of the main targets of Krylov's satire was Tsar Alexander I (1801-1825). He is the object of mockery in *Young Lion's Education, The Lion A-Hunting, Fishes Dancing,* and *Speckled Sheep.* True, *Fishes Dancing* had to be severely modified before it was allowed to be published, and *Speckled Sheep* was not published during Krylov's lifetime. These fables are not so much concerned with the Tsar's personal faults (although these are mentioned, too), but with his inadequacy as a ruler and monarch more interested in his small retinue than in the people of his country.

Young Lion's Education is one of the early fables. It alludes

to the Tsar's education which did not teach him anything about
the needs of the people. It ends with the moral:

> For him whom nature sets the beasts to regulate,
> And this the highest lore that monarch can command,
> To understand
> Your native land
> And all that makes your country great. (III, 12)

Krylov's most intense attack on Alexander is in the fable
Fishes Dancing (1824). In it the King of Beasts entrusts the
ruling of the state to a cruel and self-seeking governor who
oppresses his subjects. This is undoubtedly a reference to the
real ruler of Russia, Count Arakcheev, who created the system of military deportation of peasants and directed the excesses
of the reactionary regime. Krylov hints that King Lion is indifferent to the sufferings of the people:

> Complaints 'gainst magistrates,
> 'Gainst mighty men and 'gainst the rich
> Made Lion lose his patience.
> To inspect his realm himself he made an expedition. (VII, 24)

This is an allusion to Alexander's passion for private tours
around the country. When he meets a magistrate frying freshly
caught fish, the King of Beasts asks him whether his "fold is
content." The fawning governor answers that the fish are leaping about in the pan with joy at seeing the king.

We've come here this fine day
To welcome you our King if you should pass this way.
"And how do my folk live, is their life nice?"
"Your gracious Majesty, they say it's paradise.
Why only now they prayed for their great Squire
That your so precious life should last their full desire."
(But in the frying pan the fish kept leaping higher.)
"Then tell me why on earth," the Lion asks, advancing,
"They twist their tales about, and wag their heads so queerly?"
"Oh most wise Lion," said the man, "they're dancing
For joy because they see the King they love so dearly."

> At this the gracious Lion licked the governor's breast,
> Deigned once again to glance upon the dancing fish
> And set off on his way.* (VII, 24)

It would be difficult to imagine a more caustic satire against a monarch who is allegedly concerned about his subjects, but who, in reality, approves and supports their oppression and cruel humiliation. Krylov demonstrates the hypocrisy of the Tsar's speeches and the shameless deception of those to whom he entrusted the government.

But despite the evident allusion to specific historical figures, the main value of Krylov's fables is that their applicability is so broad. The Lion, for example, has all the typical traits of cruel, hypocritical autocrats, accustomed to fawning servility while administering justice and meting out punishment at their own discretion. Such fables as *Lion and Wolf* and *The Lion A-Hunting* deal with this subject. When the booty is being divided, the King of Beasts takes his lion's share for granted and announces:

> Now, look, my friends! You see?
> > This portion falls to me
> > > By act and deed.
> And this belongs to me as lion—that's agreed.
> And this is mine, because I'm stronger than you three.
> And as for this, the beast that puts a paw that way,
> > He won't go home alive to-day.   (IV, 16)

Speckled Sheep (1821) is equally pointed. It ridicules Alexander's hypocrisy and censures his cruel reprisals against the officers and men of the Semenovsky Regiment for mutinying in 1821 in protest against inhuman military drills and countless punishments. It could also be that the fable reflects the affair of the professors who were expelled from St. Petersburg University for being free-thinkers.

The fable tells the sad tale of some speckled sheep who stood out from ordinary sheep and gave rise to the displeasure of

---

* This version was not authorized. In the one passed by the censors, the Lion does not believe the governor and justly punishes him. The authorized version is the one given in Pares, VII, 24.

the King of Beasts. The Lion, therefore, called a council of his closest courtiers, the Bear and Fox, and complained to them that "To see a speckled sheep so hurts my eyes, I find—The sight is simply undermined." The Bear, representing the rude martinet Arakcheev, advised him "without another word" to "condemn the sheep to be destroyed." But the King did not wish to have recourse to such a blatant and bloody infringement of the law. The fox, perceiving that "the Lion frowns," gives him the cunning and hypocritical advice to take the sheep to the meadow and order the wolves to guard them. The King eagerly takes this advice. Sure enough, the speckled sheep soon disappear, and only a few of the plain sheep are left. The Lion had nothing directly to do with it, even though he managed to rid himself of the hated "speckled sheep." This was in essence what happened to the mutineering soldiers of the Semenovsky Regiment. They were sent away to distant garrisons where they soon perished from the harsh climatic conditions. The significance of the fable is broader; it is about the authorities meting out punishment to independent thinkers.

Under the cover of fictional characters, Krylov wrote the unpleasant truth about the oppression of simple working people by the titled and mighty. *The Plague of the Beasts* is about the hypocrisy of the powers that be and the injustice of a social system based on the rule of plunderers who make laws for the enslavement of the people. They turn out to be in the right even in the most "godless deeds." Plunderers who "confess" their sins come out unscathed because they themselve are the judges. The Lion expresses the sham regret, "poor little lambs—and why? they never injured me,—I've mangled piteously." But the court sycophants immediately assure him that "to the sheep great honour it must bring" when the King eats them. And when misfortune catches up with the common people, it turns out that the guilty are not the real criminals who occupy high positions—not the bears, tigers or wolves—but the mild, harmless Ox:

> The tiger next, and bear, and then the wolves in turn
> Give all to learn
> They too have got to own some foibles lilliputian;

> But all their most unrighteous deeds,
> Not one that whispers, one that heeds;
> And all the strong in claw and tooth
> Escape from this tribunal of the truth,
>   On every side
> Not only justified, but almost sanctified.   (II, 4)

The political significance of this fable is quite clear, as are Krylov's true feelings about conditions in Russia.

Abuse of power, lawlessness, and embezzlement of state property by high officials, judges, and the entire bureaucratic establishment were among the chief evils of the serf-owning state. They were harshly censured and ridiculed by Russian satirists such as Novikov, Fonvizin, Kapnist, and Gogol. The indignation of the progressive elements of society at these abuses can be judged from what Bestuzhev wrote in his notes on the reasons for the origin of the Decembrist movement: "In short, in the treasury, at law courts, at the commissariat, at the governors', at the governor-general's, wherever interest was involved, anyone who could—plundered, and he who did not dare—thieved. Nowhere did honesty pay, and informers and swindlers rejoiced."[4] Another revolutionary, Wilhelm Küchelbecker, when giving testimony at the inquest on the Decembrist affair, said that he joined the secret society because he was indignant at "the abuses which ... were prevalent in most governmental departments." He listed the negative characteristics of society against which the Decembrists had revolted: "horrible oppression of the peasants," "moral dissolution," "insufficient education," and extreme "constraint by the censorship."[5] And these are, in fact, the basic themes of Krylov's satirical fables. *The Raven Chick, Wolves and Sheep,* and *Elephant as Governor* deal with these very matters; their characters are so typical that they constitute a very real social satire. *Fox and Marmot* contains a convincing picture of a venal fox, sanctimonious and at the same time considering bribes to be part of the natural course of events:

> My friend the Inspector seems in such despair
> As if to-night the bailiffs will be there,
>   And, truly, all the town's aware

He couldn't spare a shilling for his life,
        No more his wife:
    Yet, bit by bit, just watch and wait,
He builds a little house, he buys a small estate.
Though how his income squares with what he pays away,
        You'll never prove in court, no doubt,
        Yet right or wrong, I'm sure you'll say:
        "I've noticed feathers on your snout!"   (II, 10)

In *Wolf and Lamb*, Krylov demonstrates the "right" of the
strong on the basis of the wolf's law: "Your guilt consists in
this: I want to eat you up!" Krylov took the plot from La Fontaine, but added a foreword which underlined and broadened
its socio-political significance:

        The weak, against the strong,
        Is always in the wrong.
        Of this in history, examples you may see;
            But we're not writing history;
        So here is what the fables have to say. (I, 13)

The Raven Chick describes how the notable and distinguished
plunderers who prey upon the people have minor thieves creep-
ing in their wake, though these are often caught red-handed:

I rather think for us, the example is not wasted!
        Let no small cheat
    With bigger birds of prey compete!
    Where big thieves may go free, the little ones get basted. (II, 21)

The hero of *Elephant as Governor* is one who uses his privileged position to plunder and ruin the common people. At first
he seems quite kind-hearted and as one who attempts to be
just, but his stupidity and blind faith in his officials suggest
that, for all intents and purposes, he encourages extortion and
tyranny just as much as the conscious plunderers and self-
seekers. When the "kindly ruler" receives a complaint from the
sheep that the wolves are "tearing off their skin," the elephant
calls the wolves to account for this pillage. Since they know how
stupid their governor is, the wolves find it easy to persuade him
that they will take only "for our winter dress . . . a modest contribution." The elephant reconciles himself to this:

"So that's it!" said the judge. "Well, you take care!
Injustice is a thing I can't abide;
The law allows, so take the hide!
And but for that, you're not to touch a hair!" (II, 22)

It is difficult not to agree with the author when he declares at the beginning of this fable:

Well may we dread
Strong arm, weak head;
If heart is weak as well, then count the man no good. (II, 22)

Krylov understood that arbitrary rule and lawlessness in tsarist Russia were not simply isolated manifestations of dishonesty and self-interest on the part of irresponsible officials, but the links in the whole system—the result of corruption over the entire state apparatus. *The Peasants and the River* shows astonishing understanding of the antipopular nature of these phenomena. It reveals the collusion against the people on the part of all the elements comprising the autocratic, serf-owning state. The fable tells how the peasants, disillusioned by the rivulets and streams that carry away their property during floods, go to "entreat" the River "to make their grievance good." But when they come to it, they see that "the half of what they'd lost was floating on its breast." They are convinced that it is as useless to go on to the "small," low-ranking officials for justice as to the "great," high officials, and return home dispirited:

And as they went, they said:
"It's no use wasting trouble there;
To win your suit against the small, despair,
When all their plunder with the great they share!" (IV, 18)

Wolves and Sheep, one of Krylov's last fables, gives a general picture of the lawlessness and arbitrary plundering that was characteristic of the ruling circles. It depicts the hypocrisy of the autocratic regime in protecting itself while plundering the people. When the sheep complain that they are given no peace by the wolves, "The rulers of the beasts, their best attention giving," instituted a Council for solving disputes between the wolves and the sheep. The only flaw in the plan was that the

very same wolves were to take part in the Council. The fable
concludes with a cheerless denunciation of the cynicism of tsarist
courts and the entire state apparatus:

> There's nothing left to add, and nothing to delete;
>> Only the way it works is not so good.
> For though the court, they say, is scrupulously fair,
>> The sheep may plaintiff or defendant be—
>> The dragging's never done by him, and he
> Has yet to make his first appearance there. (IX, 5)

This is the final mockery that exposes the attempts of the
authorities to justify their coercion of the people. And it is no
coincidence that Belinsky quoted this fable in its entirety in his
brilliant review of Krylov's fables.

III   *Fact and Typification*

It would, however, be a mistake to associate Krylov's fables
only with the satirization of specific events, for their full meaning is much broader than any given event. A *Quartet* will serve
as an example. Krylov was prompted to write it on the occasion
of one of Alexander I's liberal gestures—the formation in 1810
of a State Council equipped with advisory powers but whose
members were appointed by the Tsar himself. Krylov saw how
useless this enterprise was from the very beginning and mocked
it maliciously in his fable about four stupid, self-assured animals—the monkey, the ass, the goat and the clumsy-pawed bear—
who decided to form a quartet, though they did not know how to
play the instruments. They thought that the secret of playing
lay not in the skill, but in the position of the musicians:

> "Stop, boys," cries little monkey, "wait a bit;
> It can't go right like that; you don't know how to sit!
>> You face viola, bear, with your bassoon;
>> First fiddle faces second; then, you'll see,
>>> We'll play to quite another tune
>> And make the hills and forest dance for glee." (IV, I)

The unfortunate musicians are condemned mercilessly and
categorically:

The nightingale replies: "To sit, is not enough.
Besides, my friends, your ears are much too rough.
Then change your seats, and fiddles too:
Yet chamber music's not for you!" (IV, I)

This mockery of the hopeless musicians is much more than
a gibe at Alexander's ill-considered measure. The fable is applicable to any bureaucratic enterprise, incompetent self-
appointed officials, and to every situation in which untrained
and unskilled persons try to do something for which they are
not suited. Such is the wide range of the satirical significance
of this fable, that it is still relevant in our days.

When he depicts representatives of the ruling classes, Krylov
reveals in detail and in depth the social essence of their mentality. In the fable *Pop-a-Pop*, for example, he reveals the hypocrisy of a rich man ("he had stored a million in a casket") who
would "prefer a pleasant reputation." His hypocrisy makes him
put on a show of caring about the poor, but his greed is such
that he makes sure that it does not cost him anything.

Poor Rich Man shows the psychology of people obsessed with
accumulating gold aimlessly, but with frantic greed. At the
beginning of the fable, the hero is still poor and is able to
reason soundly. But from the moment he is possessed by a sense-
less passion to amass a fortune, he loses his critical faculty and
finally dies on a heap of gold coins. The description of the hero's
character is not allegorical, although the fable itself is: the
"poor rich man's" character becomes a generalization while
retaining its realistic, psychologically accurate traits.

In *The Bag* Krylov describes a typical *nouveau riche*. An empty
bag was despised by all: "The under-servants on their way would
wipe their boots upon him as they passed." Only when by happy
chance the bag became filled with gold pieces was it credited
with weight and importance. Krylov is not merely emphasizing
how typical this social phenomenon is, but manages to convey
the character of this *parvenu* in two or three strokes.

The bag puts on such airs,
Gets clever and gets uppish;
Our bag begins to talk, and talks most awful rubbish.

Lays down the law like Solon's double,
With "That won't pass!"
And "He's an ass,"
And "That, you'll see, will lead to trouble!" (III, 7)

According to Krylov, stupidity and ignorance are no obstacle for a rich man who wants to judge everything and lay down the law to all. He is certain to find obsequious listeners.

Krylov's fables are not caricatures, but typical descriptions of real life. Even when he exaggerates some negative trait, he does not make his character lose his lifelike qualities. On the contrary, the hyperbole helps to reflect the typical social phenomenon all the more vividly and gives the character traits that are more general.

In the fable *The Ass and his Bell* Krylov expresses the people's contempt for stupid high officials who consider that their merits and rights lie in the ranks and decorations, which they have received undeservedly. The Aesopic language does not tone down the animal's behavior, but, on the contrary, enhances the description. The Ass's new "rank" brings him only sorrow, because he can no longer misbehave as he used to without drawing attention to himself. The moral of the fable underlines how typical this situation is:

In public life, as oft we see,
The rogue must count on this! While poor and low his station,
He may escape your observation;
But honors on a rogue are like a bell:
The sounds they make go far, and loud the tale they tell. (VIII, 13)

Pike is bitter satire on tsarist law courts where the real bribe-takers and thieves go unpunished. Krylov mocks both the magistrates and the bureaucratic legal procedure itself. The judges are two asses, two old nags, and two or three goats. This venomously contemptuous description shows that the "magistrates" had long since not been used for anything. According to rumor, the public prosecutor, the Fox, has been bribed by the Pike ("Pike supplied the fish for Doctor Fox's board") and has, therefore, thought up a ruse to save the Pike from punishment for "wronging all the fishy tribe." The comic effect is enhanced by the animals talking and behaving like real court officials. The Pike's crimes are so blatant that

> The Justices went on, their sentence thus to fix:—
> To deal the death of shame that is his due
> And hang him on a bough, that such may see and rue. (VIII, 5)

The Fox's resourceful speech relies on his listener's deliberate stupidity and long lost ability to reason. He employs the stereotyped formulas of court rhetoric:

> "Your Worships on the Bench," the Fox puts in his nose:
> "To hang is not enough; I venture to propose
>   A punishment unheard of—strange and new!—
> That criminals henceforth may tremble and take heed,
> Let's drown him in the stream!" "That's excellent indeed,"
> The magistrates exclaimed; and being all agreed,
>   Into the stream that pike they threw.   (VIII, 5)

Krylov wrote his last fable *A Great Lord* in 1834. It clearly shows that he had lost neither his satirical keenness nor his poetic gifts. Belinsky thought particularly highly of this fable because of its "power and freshness," and quoted it in full in his review of the 1843 edition of Krylov's fables. It describes the judgement in the world of the dead of a deceased satrap. When Aeacus suggests that this selfish idler be sent to paradise, Mercury, the messenger of the gods, protests: "Atrocious! I object." Upon which Aeacus answers ironically:

> "Why, can't you understand? This Satrap was a fool!
>   What, if possessed of so much power,
>   Himself in some unlucky hour
>   Had tried his satrapy to rule?
> He would have wrecked the province, caused to fall
> A flood of tears that could not be forgiven!" (IX, 11)

The satire in this fable was so sharp and relevant to contemporary life that the censorship did not allow its publication for two years. It was widely circulated in manuscript form until Krylov succeeded in having it published. It is hardly likely that the satrap was meant to represent anyone in particu-

lar. It was a satire of the whole system of limitless power held
by tsarist officials.

The Eastern flavor in *A Great Lord,* just as in Voltaire, is
only a screen to hide criticism of the system of arbitrary rule
and privileges which were distributed not according to merit,
but favoritism or membership in the ruling classes.

Krylov's fables are not confined to poking fun at particular
individuals or describing specific facts. The incidents which
impelled him to write the fables have long been forgotten, but
the general meaning of the satire has survived.

IV   *Misconceptions*

Krylov's fables come to the sad conclusion that in a serf-
owning, bureaucratic state the people cannot escape being
oppressed and defrauded of their natural rights. *Beasts in Council*
has the following lines:

> Whatever rules you may devise,
> Once put them in the hands of men that have no conscience,
> The part which most to them applies
> They're sure to find some trick for turning into nonsense (IV, 20)

Despite the fabulist's rather moderate views and his great care
not to "tease" the noble "geese," many of Krylov's fables refer
to completely negative features of contemporary life. At the
same time, however, he wrote about the hopelessness of political
change and was ready to reconcile himself to the glaring imperfections of the tsarist régime for fear that some other new rule
might be even worse for the people (see *The Frogs Ask for a
King*). This was the source of his political scepticism and his
distrust of various innovations, liberal projects, and talk about
reforms which were so fashionable at the beginning of Alexander I's reign, but none of which helped the people in the least.

Thus, alongside the critical fables, we see fables which attack
the radical ideas put forward by the French Revolution of
1789 (*Horse and Rider, A Blade of Corn, Author and Robber,*
etc.). He sees in them cause for anxiety and a resulting moral
corruption which destroys the moral principles he considers

unshakable. In *Author and Robber* Krylov has the revolutionary
events in France in mind when he accuses the Author of preach-
ing anarchic and immoral principles:

> Who mocked at government and marriage vow,
>   In law a childish dream did find,
> Set down to these alone all woes that scourge our kind,
> And strove the social bond to tear asunder? Thou. (VI, 24)

His fear of revolutionary upheavals and his political moderation limited the breadth of ideas in his satire. Although he
censured the tyranny and cruel autocracy of the Tsar and
his entourage, he did not go so far as to oppose the monarchical
system itself, for he believed that an enlightened monarch
could reform an unjust and lawless society by his rational
behavior and respect for the law. Another reason for his not
having radical views was his fear that there would be a repetition of a peasant uprising similar to the Pugachev Rebellion
of 1772-74, the memories of which had haunted Krylov since
childhood. This explains why some of his fables attack revolutionary strivings. For example, *Horse and Rider* tells how a
horse suddenly longed for freedom, threw his rider, "And there
was crushed," when it fell. Krylov comes to the disheartening
conclusion:

> Let freedom's charms be ne'er so fair,
>   For peoples yet
> There's no less harm and danger there,
> Where no wise limit has been set. (IV, 17)

But, if in order to avoid anarchy one must observe a limit,
then there is nothing left but reconciliation with the system.
And so, in *A Blade of Corn* Krylov implies that all people must
reconcile themselves to their position in the state. The allegory
is that of a blade of corn which grumbles that the master pays
it little attention, whereas the flowers in the greenhouse are
pampered and kept warm.

> Thus oft some honest countryman,
> Plain soldier, simple artisan,

With some one else compares his situation,
And grumbles at his lowly station.
'Tis something like my tale might serve as explanation. (VI, 20)

The Shepherd and the Sea tells of a shepherd who was enticed by the possibility of making his fortune by investing all his property in goods which were to be sold abroad. Unfortunately, the ship on which the goods were loaded perished in a storm. Having learned from bitter experience, the shepherd is no longer willing to risk his belongings, but rejoices in his modest way of life: "Far better guard what's yours for sure/ Than follow in the wake of Hope's deceptive lure!" (VI, 15).

This call for moderation was Krylov's substitute for fighting against the system.

These last mentioned fables were not only a deviation from the generally democratic trends of his writings, but were a renunciation of his literary achievements, being didactic abstract allegories. Some were written for official readings to celebrate the Public Library's anniversaries, others—to protect himself against suspicion on the part of the authorities.

V   *Literary Polemic*

Krylov's fables are often a commentary on the literature of his time. He ridicules the narrowness and smugness even of those literary groups to which he himself belonged ("Society of the Lovers of the Russian Word"). The fable *Parnassus* (1808) is an attack against the Russian Academy in which the tone was set by advocates of an already obsolete Classicism, led by Admiral Alexander Shishkov, an ardent defender of Old Church Slavonic. Krylov's relations with the Russian Academy were rather strained. A year later, in 1809, he failed to be elected a member, possibly because of *Parnassus.*

This fable mocks the attempts of untalented poets to "form a choir" and conquer Parnassus. The asses who graze on Parnassus "somehow came to know that Muses lived there long ago." One of them summons the others.

"... No shyness, boys! 'twould be absurd!
We'll chant the glories of our herd;

> Louder, ay, louder than the sisters nine,
> We'll form the asses' choir and raise our hymn divine.
> And if some wilful voice outside our canons passes,
> We'll keep this golden rule, which ass-like I may call:—
> Whoever has a voice that fails to please us asses,
> He shall not sing up here at all." (I, 8)

And just in case there was still doubt as to whom the fable had as a target, Krylov makes the ass express himself in the archaic language of Shishkov and his followers: "This cunning, quaint and curious speech/ Appealed in ass-like way to each." *Parnassus*, a virulent, topical polemic, subsequently lost its sting and acquired a more general meaning which is expressed in the moral:

> I hope no ass my nose will pull,
> If with a trite remark I end this fable;
> Once you have an empty skull,
> No post you get will make it full.

The greater the scope of the fable, the longer it lasts. But Krylov achieved breadth of meaning not only by means of allegorical symbolism, which in principle can be understood only on one level, but by creating realistic characters who, while preserving their specific qualities, are endowed with a great deal of substance and artistic vividness.

Ass and Nightingale acquired its generalized meaning in a curious way. V. Kenevich, who obtained information from persons who knew Krylov, writes:

A certain official (according to some, Count A. K. Razumovsky, according to others, Count A. N. Golitsyn) . . . invited him to his house and asked him to read two or three fables. Krylov read a few fables with artistry, including one he had borrowed from La Fontaine. The official listened favorably to them and then said thoughtfully: "That was good, but why do you not translate like Ivan Dmitriev?" "I don't know how to," the poet answered modestly. And here the dialogue ended. When he got home, stung to the quick, Krylov gave vent to his bile in the fable, *Ass and Nightingale*.[6]

Whether true or not, this story is not essential to the understanding of *Ass and Nightingale*. The phenomenon described here is such a general one that the actual prototype or event does not affect the understanding or application of the character in the fable. The fable is a stinging gibe at self-assured and, at the same time, ignorant dignitaries, who are confident that they are connoisseurs of the arts. Not surprisingly, the ass's pretensions to be a judge of art and set standards offend the really inspired artist. Krylov emphasizes the contrast between the nightingale's song at the sound of which "The breezes sank to rest; the choirs of birds were stilled" with the uncouth, patronizing tone of the ass as he deigns to praise the nightingale:

> It ceased, and nodding grave, the ass his judgment gave:
> "Not bad at all," he said; "in fact, my boy,
> It's music one can quite enjoy.
> But how your heart would warm
> To hear our cock perform!
> Just think of all the tricks you'd learn
> If for a hint or two, to him you'd turn." (II, 23)

The ass's vulgar taste and ignorance are exposed by his own words.

Cock and Cuckoo (1834) is pointed literary satire aimed at Faddey V. Bulgarin and Nikolay I. Grech, two reactionary writers and journalists hated by all progressive intellectuals. It was they who used to sing each other's praises shamelessly in the newspapers and journals they published themselves. This fable is evidence that Krylov's genius had not flagged, nor had the sharpness of his satire lost its edge. Written during the literary and social controversy of the 1830's it was, therefore, one of the most topical of his fables. Krylov was anticipated in this theme by Pushkin who had written one of his witty parodies in 1831, in which he castigated Bulgarin and Grech equally for their enraptured references to each other.

The targets of Krylov's fable were made all the more clear to contemporaries because the fable was accompanied by a caricature of the cuckoo and the cock whose faces were easily recognizable as those of Bulgarin and Grech. The significance of the fable is, however, much broader than the mere ridicule of two men: it is about anyone who indulges in mutual flattery for ulterior motives.

Krylov never revealed the source of his fables, a fact which distressed one of his contemporaries: "Krylov never told anyone what prompted him to write any of his fables, but if a close friend made a guess, he would deny it in such a way that his denial could be taken for a confirmation. 'Could be and very likely is' or 'Just a coincidence!' he would say."[7] He did this not only to avoid trouble, but because he had a true understanding of the fabulist's genre as a means of exposing typical manifestations of reality and not just separate facts. For, if a fable goes no further than describing an isolated fact, it is an indication that the author is untalented, and the fable is a failure, condemned to a short life.

A. A. Potebnya said: "The effect of a fable on particular phenomena which stand in need of generalization can be compared to salt solution in a salt-lake when it condenses, and the chips and twigs in it serve as a base for the formation of crystals."[8]

This is what makes the fable one of the most difficult genres in which to write. It demands maximum economy and the strictest selection of literary details; it must be entirely free of superfluous detail, and all the particular facts must become crystals which form its general meaning.

CHAPTER 5

The Genre and Tradition of Fable

I *The Evolution of the Fable*

THE fable is one of the oldest literary genres. Aesop wrote his fables in the 6th-5th century B.C. The collection of old Indian sayings and fables under the title of *Panchatantra* date back to the 3rd and 4th centuries A.D. The Middle Ages also had their fable writers. Aesop's fables were first translated into Russian during the reign of Peter I.

Russia did not develop its own original fables, however, before the beginning of the eighteenth century, but in the middle of the eighteenth century a pleiad of fabulists had made their appearance. "Russia has been particularly fortunate in her fables," wrote Belinsky. But, when he went through the numerour Russian fabulists he came to the conclusion that "the fable owes its true triumph to Krylov. He is our only genuine and great fabulist."[1]

The fable has retained its structural basis right up to our time. This does not mean, however, that the genre itself has not undergone any changes. Its long history saw many alterations, from the allegory of the ancients to today's realistic satire. But these changes were made against the background of the traditional form.

The ancient fables of Aesop were abstract allegories followed by a didactic moral. The action and characters were schematic, and the narrative was devoid of realistic elements and details. The fables dwelt only on the main points in the plot; they were a kind of libretto which outlined the plot. There was almost no dialogue, only general logical formulas. Krylov's fables were in complete contrast to these. His were miniature comedy scenes depicting everyday life, outstanding for the vitality of their characters and the wealth and diversity of their language.

In order to convey the difference between Krylov's fables and those of Aesop we need take only one example: Let us compare Krylov's *Crow and Fox* with the corresponding fable by Aesop, *Raven and Fox*. Of course, La Fontaine's fable of the same name comes between, and Krylov's fable is immeasurably closer to it than to Aesop's, but we are now not so much considering the historical question of its literary genesis as comparing the actual *type* of fable.

Aesop's fable goes like this:

A raven carried away a piece of meat and perched in a tree. A fox saw him and wanted to have the meat for himself. He stood before the raven and set about flattering him: How big he was and how beautiful, and how he would be better fitted than others to be the King of the Birds and, indeed, would become king if he also had a voice. The raven felt like showing the fox that he did have a voice; he let go of the meat and emitted a loud croak. The fox, meanwhile, ran up, snatched the meat and said: "Ah, raven, if only you also had a brain in your head, then you would have all the requirements to become king."[2]

Krylov took this plot (after La Fontaine) and wrote the following:

How often have they told us, please,
And always to no use—that flattery's mean and base?
The flatterer in our hearts will always find a place.
God somehow sent the crow a little bit of cheese.
    The crow had perched upon a fir.
She seemed to have settled down to enjoy her provender,
But mused with mouth half-closed, the dainty bit still in it.
Unhappily the fox came running past that minute:
A whiff of scent soon brings him to a pause,
And Reynard sights the cheese, and Reynard licks his jaws.
The rascal steals on tip-toe to the tree,
He curls his tail and, gazing earnestly,
He speaks so soft, scarce whispering each word:
"How beautiful you are, sweet bird!
What a neck, and oh! what eyes,
Like a dream of Paradise!
Then, what feathers! what a beak!
And, sure, an angel's voice if only you would speak!

Sing, darling; don't be shy! Oh, sister, truth to tell,
If you, with charms like these, can sing as well,
Of birds you'd be the queen adorable!"
The silly creature's head turns giddy with his praise;
    Her breath, for very rapture, swells her throat;
    The fox's soft persuasion she obeys,
And high as crow can pitch she caws one piercing note.
Down falls the cheese!—Both cheese and fox have gone their ways.
                                           (I, 1)

It can be clearly seen that Aesop's fable plot has been transformed. Krylov took its bare outline and endowed it with bright colors, embroidering it with variegated word patterns. Krylov's crow is a different type from Aesop's raven. It is not an abstract allegorical bird, but conceited, self-loving, stupid, and susceptible to blatant flattery. His fox is clever and ingratiating; he despises the foolish crow and knows very well how he can cheat her. The dialogue is marvelously expressive, as is the very fabric of the fable. The fox is superbly rhetorical, flattering the crow with inspiration, drawing his vocabulary from popular speech. His power of seduction lies in the folktale quality of his flattering speech.

When Pushkin said that Krylov and La Fontaine expressed the spirit of their people, he was talking about the national peculiarities which the fable acquired in French and Russian literatures. Whereas, the ancient fable inclined to a logically abstract discourse, La Fontaine's and Krylov's fables were famed more for their literary inventiveness and their very poetic manner. La Fontaine retained many of Aesop's plots, but used them as a canvas on which to create poetical scenes and pictures. In the foreword to the first collection of his fables, La Fontaine wrote: "I took into consideration the fact that since everyone knows these fables I can renovate them by only touching them up a little for the sake of elegance."[3]

In Russia, the fable-writing tradition, characterized by an interest in familiar plots and the creation of individual poetical styles, was enriched by an interest in folklore and the vulgar, "low" literature which began in the eighteenth century and continued the traditions of the *skomorokhs* (buffoons). Alexander Sumarokov's literary activity in the eighteenth century introduced into the Russian tradition of fable writing those features from the common people which were used with such good effect by Krylov. Krylov drew on folk tradition and strove to make the fable not an elegant tableau or an amusing scene, but a realistic portrayal of life, conveying a typical image and entailing a moral or satirical conclusion. This is what distinguishes his fables from La Fontaine's, even though they are both based on the same plots.

The fable is first and foremost an allegory which teaches a moral. This moral is the most important element in the fables of Aesop, Gotthold E. Lessing, and their followers, but it is hidden amid details from real life in those of La Fontaine and Krylov.

The history of the fable can be divided into two branches. The first includes the allegorical parables of Aesop and later, in the eighteenth century, Lessing and his followers. This type is devoid of expressiveness and color. It is usually written in prose and, in Lessing's words: "ought to be marked by the sparing simplicity of the ancient fable." He considered that there was no greater sin than the poetical paintings of La Fontaine's fables. "The narrative of a fable," wrote Lessing, "ought to be simple and condensed, and serve only the interests of clarity, avoiding as far as possible any sort of varnishing or figure of speech."[4]

La Fontaine's method of writing, the second branch in the development of the fable, was the direct opposite of Lessing's, and full of the "varnishing" that Lessing hated so much. Lessing believed that poetical expressiveness destroyed the philosophical and allegorical character of the fable, drowned it, and deprived it of its main quality—simplicity and allegorical significance. He compared La Fontaine, who was the first to write poetical fables, to a hunter who asked a painter to carve a hunting scene on his bow. When the time came to use the bow, the hunter drew it, and it snapped. Lessing considered that poetical beauty was incompatible with the practical purpose of fables and that the more artistic the fable, the less it fulfilled its purpose.

Krylov left no theoretical discourses on the fable, but all his writings oppose this point of view. He followed in La Fontaine's steps, repudiating the asceticism both of Lessing and of the ancient fable. Krylov most often adapted La Fontaine's plots. Only as an exception did he turn directly to Aesop for his plot, and Lessing is used only once (*The Godless Tribe*).

II   *The Russian Fable*

The fable held a place of honor in Russian literature of the eighteenth century. Antioch Kantemir, Mikhail Lomonosov, and Vasily Trediakovsky were the pioneers of the fable in Russia which flourished in the 1760's, becoming one of the most popular genres of poetry. Alexander Sumarokov, a vivid and original Russian fabulist, determined the direction of the genre for a long time to come. He was the first to imbue it with national character, linking it with folklore, folk tales, jokes, and proverbs. He even took his plots from folklore rather than from Aesop or La Fontaine. The somewhat coarse humor of his parables, often based on an everyday scene, as well as the practical moral, revealed national traits. The sharp changes in the rhythm of the line, the conversational tone, the continued change in the number of feet per line (ranging from six-foot lines to two-foot and even one-foot), and the buoyant popular speech were all new to the genre, and paved the way for a truly Russian fable, closely linked with its folklore sources. Sumarokov's fables soon became generally popular and were widely read. This popularization was facilitated by printing them in cheap, mass editions with illustrations by self-taught artists.

For Sumarokov, the fable was a "low," burlesque genre in which he could treat crude things with contemptuous superiority. He found his plots in the common peasant's life, and described his animals in the same style: "Two rats met at a drinking house/ And bawled and yelled all night:/ They sang rough bargemen's songs with all their might."[5] (Two Rats)

In his descriptions of peasant life and morals, Sumarokov endowed his animals with qualities characteristic of peasants and petty officials. For him, the peasant was a comic butt, and he delighted in making fun of his coarseness and ignorance. Though he led the way to the realistic fable, he was not able to create the genuinely popular art of the fable which Krylov was to do later.

Krylov learned much from Sumarokov, although he did not adopt his grotesque, crude style. The main point they had in common was their immersion in everyday life; they both made the fable a lively scene, repudiating the abstract qualities of the allegory. Another similarity was in their use of popular conversational speech with its peasant humor. Nonetheless, Krylov's fables have a totally different character. They are more general in their meaning, wiser, and more realistic. The grotesque and crude features of Sumarokov's fables are alien to Krylov. In his depiction of everyday life, Krylov is by no means a portrayer of morals and manners. He is concerned with describing types, making his meaning general and his images realistic.

Sumarokov's style proved to be contagious, and he was followed by a number of writers: Vasily Maykov, Alexey A. Rzhevsky, and others.

The next stage in the development of the Russian fable is associated with the name of Ivan I. Khemnitser (1745-84). He was German by origin and was closely linked with the traditions of the German literature of the Enlightenment. He was particularly influenced by Christian Fürchtegott Gellert, a philosopher and fabulist of the Enlightenment, whose fables he elaborated in Russian. Khemnitser is incomparably drier and more didactic in style than Sumarokov. He looks at life through the eyes of a man of the Enlightenment, deeming moral standards, criteria of honesty, moderation, and virtue to be the most important features in a fable. His fables are more philosophical, the setting of everyday life loses its importance, and their basis is abstract allegory. His merit is that he introduced the fable into literature not through the back door, but as a full-fledged poetical genre. As a representative of the Russian Enlightenment, Khemnitser treated the fable as a didactic genre which could be a vehicle for propagating the main ideas of the Enlightenment. The fable was no longer a "low," plebeian genre as it was for Sumarokov and his followers, but a means of communicating philosophical ideas. However, Khemnitser's fables were much impoverished by their abstractness, rationalism, and bookishness.

All these stages in the development of the Russian fable were clearly distinguished by Alexey Merzlyakov, a poet and literary critic of the beginning of the nineteenth century: "Sumarokov found them among the simple, lower-class people; Khemnitser brought them to the town; and Dmitriev opened the doors for them to the enlightened and educated society, distinguished for its taste and language."[6]

Thus, Krylov's fables did not appear out of a vacuum, but were the result of much productive work by his predecessors. He combined Sumarokov's colorful liveliness and humor with Khemnitser's philosophy and sobriety. Indeed, he went further and created a fable which knew no equal in Realism and inexhaustible variety. It became the forerunner of the powerful Russian Realistic literature of the nineteenth century. At the same time he put an end to the Classicists' classification of the fable as a low genre. But he kept the structure of the fable, for if it had no moral, it could no longer be called a fable. The fable lost this structural principle with the writers of the Sentimentalist School, when it turned into either an elegy (by Ivan Dmitriev) or an album sketch (by Vasily Zhukovsky).

But the fable is a rigid genre, and its didactic aim determines the structural principle. Krylov's fables remained fables even though they acquired artistic qualities, because he did not change this principle. Whatever artistic content his scenes and tableaux may have, they still always preserve their moral lesson. Thus, his fables can be enjoyed on two levels: at their face value as lively stories, or as moral tales.

Krylov added realism to the fable. He not only gave more consistency to its background of everyday life, but turned it into a lively dramatic scene. Belinsky wrote: "... Krylov's fables are not simply fables: they are tales, comedies, humorous sketches, malicious satire, in short what you will, but not simply fables."[7]

III   *The Structure of the Fable*

The fable is made up of two parts: a descriptive tale—the "picture," and a didactic moral. La Fontaine wrote in the foreword to his fables that "The apologue consists of two parts which may be called, one, the body, and the other, the soul. The body is the fable and the soul is the moral."[8]

The interrelation between the two components of the fable can be expressed in various ways. In some cases the "soul" is hidden in the "body" and must be inferred from the very action of the fable. In others, it is expressed independently in the form of a didactic moral as a conclusion to the fable.

"The fable is the poetry of reason," according to Belinsky. A fable's didactic purpose is the basis for the genre's structure. Belinsky saw in Krylov's fables their own particular type of poetry: "Now this is real comedy! And at the same time it is pervaded with clear reason and common sense which is present in the poetry for the very purpose of sprinkling it with rays of wit and sparkling it with the pyrotechnics of jokes and humor."[9]

The moral expresses the opinion of the fabulist that makes the meaning of the fable generally applicable. Such is the case with the moral of *Crow and Fox*, which precedes the plot of this fable ("How often have they told us, please.").

The exhortation or moral which can be inferred from the fable and comprises its "soul," is the "lesson" that the author wants us to learn by presenting it graphically in the plot through the characters.

It is usually impossible and even undesirable to try to ferret out the one specific incident that led Krylov to write any given fable. The reduction of the content and moral of a fable to an isolated event signifies a refusal to understand its general significance. Let us take the fable, *Sammy's Coat*, as an example. Commentators have continuously tried to explain it as a jibe at landowners who keep mortgaging their estates without succeeding in the long run in saving themselves from total bankruptcy. But it is clear that the satirical meaning of this fable is considerably broader, directed at all frivolous and impractical people who attempt to avoid trouble by hasty and unreliable means.

The famous Russian linguist A. A. Potebnya wrote: "The allegorical tale of a fable serves to condense many single incidents to which it applies." To the question: "How can one

explain the fact that it [the fable] lives for thousands of years?"
Potebnya replied: "The explanation is that it constantly finds
ever new applications."[10] The "single incident" in a fable acquires
an unlimited meaning and generalization which makes it possible
to apply the fable to numerous similar incidents. The fabulist
takes a single, concrete fact, picks out and emphasizes its essential point, and makes a moral judgment about it. If the fable
is a good one, the moral judgment will have an aura of justice
and truth about it.

This is what comprises the wisdom of the fabulist and guaran-
tees his fables a long life. Consider Krylov's fable, *The Frogs
Ask for a King*, derived from La Fontaine's *Les Grenouilles qui
demandent un Roi*, in its turn derived from Aesop. The fable is
about a ruler's despotism and the cruel terror with which he
retains power. It made its first appearance in ancient Greece
and kept its satirical significance to the time of Krylov when
it alluded to the Russian tsar's unlimited powers. Krylov's version in particular has a specific method of typification and
generalization based on a combination of rationalistic generalization and an empirical description of everyday life. The fact
which lies at the base of a fable may be related to a single event,
but according to the rules of fable writing, it acquires generality
and can be applied to a number of analogical cases. At the same
time, the fable retains a didactic principle, "the moral," so
characteristic of works of the Realism of the Enlightenment.
The characters of the fable represent certain moral qualities of
people whose actions are strictly judged by the author of the
fable.

The moral lesson is an essential part of the fable, for the fable
is a didactic genre even if it is satirical in content. The moral
is not only in the conclusion or in the preface—although these
may be absent—but it is always in the very plot and images of
the fable, because its satirical attack is also an affirmation of a
particular moral position taken by the author.

Krylov often leaves out a separate moral, but this does not
mean that the fable is without didactic content. The moral can
be expressed in different ways. One way is the abstract allegory
characteristic of the ancient fable and the fable of the eight-

eenth century—Lessing, Gellert, and Khemnitser. The other is the method La Fontaine and Krylov used, with the moral conveyed not directly, but by revealing the essence of realistic characters.

In abandoning the purely allegorical type of fable, Krylov effected a revolution in the development of the genre. His fables are realistic pictures of life containing a wealth of meaning, including concealed condemnation, and implications of a vast range of phenomena. He uses the convention of animal characters or real people to depict events which show how humans interact. It often happens that the moral drawn by the author considerably narrows its true meaning.

The fable, *Frog and Bullock*, relates how it occurred to a conceited frog to compare itself with a bullock. The frog, of course, bursts after trying to puff itself up, and Krylov adds his judgment which presents one of a number of possible applications of the fable:

> She's not the first, and not the last;
> No wonder, when the little shopman tries
> To match the splendour of the Provost's board,
> And Hodge the farmer's son spends money like a lord. (I, 6)

It is clear that the meaning of this fable is not confined to this narrow formula. The frog that meets this wretched end is not, by any means, limited to representing those who want to pass off as "lords." It could be those who live beyond their means, or those who want to be taken for other than what they are. The fable is about the pernicious effect of vainglory in general.

Let us compare one of Krylov's fables with a corresponding one by Ivan I. Khemnitser, *Green Ass*, the plot of which he borrowed from Gellert. It relates how an ass painted green was led through the town and how the townfolk were astonished at the sight:

> A fool once led his ass along the streets for show;
> The old who saw him, and the young,
> The tall men and the small,
> Wherever they might be, shouted: "Oh, what an ass!"[11]

Gellert's and Khemnitser's fables condemn idle curiosity. They are didactic and in effect lack veracity.

Krylov took this plot and wrote the *Elephant and Pug* which sparkles with details from real life:

> An elephant was walking round the town;
>   They showed him up and down;
>   With us, it's seldom that an elephant one meets,
>   And all the loafers crowded in the streets. (III, 4)

The very first line, "An elephant was walking round the town" is so simple and conversational that it turns the incident into an absolutely natural event. But Krylov included in his fable the didactic episode about a conceited pug that barked at the elephant. Of course, the dog saw that its bark went unnoticed by the elephant:

> "Now, neighbour, stop that fooling, do!"
> Says mastiff: "Elephants are too big game for you.
> You yap, and on he goes without the slightest flurry,
>   Or worry,
> And—bark, for all you're worth—he won't even glance your way."

But it was barking at the elephant merely for the sake of barking, so that the pug could later boast:

> "Of course," says Pug, and looks most knowing;
> "That's just the hope that keeps me going,
> Without the mildest kind of fight to pass,
>   For real wild beast, first class . . ."

The moral needs no further explanation; it is made quite clear by the vivid treatment of the characteres in the fable.

The fable is like a coiled spring: as it unwinds it strikes for one target—the exposition of a didactic proposition in the form of a metaphor.

IV *The Fable as a Portrayal of Life*

Krylov often endows ordinary events with a special meaning. His fable *The Fly and the Coach,* for example, gives a typical

portrayal of customs. The didactic aspect recedes into the background and the main point of the fable is its description of a
landlord's family, with accurate comments on the relationships
between its members.

The fable begins with a description of a horse-drawn coach
dragging up a sandy hillock. This is not any old coach for the
sake of allegory, but an old-fashioned, family four-in-hand:

> 'Twas mid-day in July, as sultry as could be;
> And up a hillock deep with sand
> The squire and all his family
> A heavy four-in-hand
> Was dragging. (III, 17)

The vivid portrayal is enhanced by the rhythmical formation
of the lines, conveying how the coach was being dragged up the
hill.

The fable continues in the same vein. There is a description
of a frivolous master who goes into the forest with a pretty
maid servant to "pick mushrooms," and of a sentimental provincial lady who willingly listens to the declarations of a young
schoolteacher during this unexpected break in the journey.
Krylov pokes fun at all these goings on:

> The servants trail behind, and drone about the weather;
> The tutor and Miss Rose in whispers talk together;
> And Master is not there to lead them as he should,—
> The maid and he are gone for mushrooms to the wood.

Even the fly is no mere insubstantial allegory, but is endowed
with its own particular characteristics: "To urge the passengers
to make themselves of use/ He bustles in and out, like buyer
at a fair..."

We are presented with a realistic picture of everyday life,
the moral of which is inferred naturally from the events and not
forced out of them. The addition of an express moral at the end
of the fable, therefore, seems superfluous: "And how we wish
those idiots were more rare,/ Who feel that they must poke
their noses everywhere/ And press their useless help, where no
one asks at all!"

Krylov makes use of the grotesque in accordance with the traditions of fable writing. Thus Miss Monkey tries on spectacles without understanding their true purpose (*Miss Monkey and Her Spectacles*). Equally grotesque is the pike's mouse hunt (*Pike and Cat*) which ends with the mice gnawing off the pike's tail. And even though the comic situation is based on a historical fact—Admiral Pavel V. Chichagov's failure for letting Napoleon escape with the remainder of his troops at the Berezina River—the method of telling it is grotesque and fantastic. The Pike arranges to go hunting mice with the cat. When the cat expresses his misgivings about the pike's competency, the pike gives the self-assured reply: "What stuff you talk, dear boy! That mice my wits should tax!/ What me! that caught the sticklebacks!" (II, 16)

The very fact that the fabulous beasts talk and feel like humans sets a grotesque atmosphere by removing conventional preconceptions.

The comic effect of *Two Dogs* is based on the interplay of two levels of understanding. When the Toy boasts to the Hound, her words can be understood as a description of the idle life of the nobility:

> I live in luxury and state;
> I eat and drink off silver plate,
> And play on Master's lap, and when that fancy's gone,
> The sofa and the floor are nice to roll upon. (VII, 22)

Krylov's fables were so realistic that the critics sometimes lost sight of the fact that they were meant to be satirical and grotesque. He was often accused of not making them true to life. Thus, in the following lines in *Elephant as Governor*, the wolves justify themselves before their governor: "You let us, for our winter dress,/ Collect from all the sheep a modest contribution" (II, 22). A critic during Krylov's time had this comment to make: "What do wolves need sheepskin coats for and are the sheepskins really necessary to them?"[12]

The fabulist, Alexander E. Izmaylov, mocked at the line from the fable *The Hare A-hunting*, "A tuft of Bruin's ear was given him in the end," by saying "Just as wolves do not eat cabbage, so hares do not feed on animal flesh."[13]

In the twentieth century the Russian naturalist Timiryazev expressed indignation that in the fable *Leaves and Roots* Krylov considered the leaves useless to trees and he even demonstrated that leaves are no less necessary for providing trees with oxygen than are roots.

These and similar reproaches have no justification, for the characters and images in the fables are grotesque and cannot be subjected to the rules of scientific verisimilitude.

CHAPTER 6

The Poetry of Fables

I *The Fable as a Comedy*

WHILE retaining the allegorical principle in the fable, Krylov usually wrote about typical, real characters. There are exceptions among his fables, however, where there are such allegorical figures as Fortune, or where the whole fable is purely allegorical, such as *The Pearl Divers.*

The fables are first and foremost meant for oral reading— they come to life when they are heard. This is not surprising when we remember that Krylov's first interest was the theater. This interest shows in the scenic qualities of his fables which determine their artistic structure. Not only is there an abundance of monologues and dialogues in his fables, but they generally serve to reveal the speakers' character; the author makes use of little scenes which are miniature comedies composed according to the rules of a work of drama.

A good illustration of this is the fable *Fox and Marmot* written in the form of a dialogue between the two animals: " 'Whither away so fast, and in such trepidation?'/ Fox asked a Marmot passing by" (II, 10).

The Fox's speech is a cunning lie of a bribe-taking bureaucrat who has been caught embezzling and who has almost come to believe sincerely that he is being wrongly persecuted:

> "Oh dear true friend," was the reply,
> "I'm slandered and disgraced, dismissed for peculation.
> You know they made me judge among the poultry kind,
> I lavished on that work my health and peace of mind,
>   Took hardly time to snatch a bite,
>   Went short of sleep each night;
>   Then, out you go, and serve you right!

> It's all a cruel lie; you too will realise
> That no one's honor's safe, if once we go by lies.
> Me peculate? Why, have I lost all sense?
> I'll put the case to you: take any evidence;
> Is that the sort of thing that I should do?
> You've only got to think it out!"

The Marmot's concluding answer immediately puts everything into perspective and exposes the Fox's lie:

> "A lie, of course," says Marmot, "though several times, it's true
> I've noticed feathers on your snout." (II, 10)

Belinsky wrote about this fable:

> Would one need to alter many lines or words in this fable to include
> it as a scene in a comedy by Griboedov, if Griboedov had written
> a comedy called *The Bribe Taker?* One would only need to change
> the animals' names to human names and also change the last line
> out of respect for the bribe-takers, for though they are knaves they
> do have faces and not snouts.[1]

One of Krylov's main achievements as a fabulist was to have
created individual characters. Ever since Aesop the animals in
fables had spoken with the voices of their authors. Each one
had acquired its specific moral attributes.

The fable does not have the element of pure fantasy which
the fairy tale has. It is a rational tale and its animals behave
not as fantastic figures and symbols, but as incarnations of
human traits and desires. The fable's descent from the beast
epic is scarcely felt, for the animals have become a kind of
symbol with the significance of each deeply rooted in the tradition of fable writing. This aspect of the fable was noted by
Vasily K. Tredyakovsky, a Russian Classicist theoretician:

> And truly, the Creator, wishing to teach man the nature of things,
> gave the animals various dispositions and characteristics so that they
> should all take the place of condensed descriptions of various duties
> which man must fulfill; and he endowed them with good and bad
> qualities which he must emulate or seek to avoid. Thus, he created
> a sensible likeness of gentleness, impudence, predatoriness, and cruelty
> in the Wolf, Lion, Tiger, and so on.[2]

Tredyakovsky states the case for purely allegorical characters, moral symbols whose role is known in advance, having been established by tradition. Krylov, on the other hand, preserves their traditional qualities to a certain extent, but transcends the convention and breathes life into the fable characters. This is what made it possible to include both human and animal characters in the fables and, in some cases (in La Fontaine, Krylov, and Gellert), to replace the animals altogether with humans. But even the human characters were, on the whole, conventional personifications of some moral or social quality. Krylov's merit is that he avoided having the characters become abstractions by endowing them with lifelike characteristics and showing them in a concrete social milieu.

The fable figures have still another structural principle, namely, that their conventional nomenclature makes it possible to make the shortest possible characterization. Potebnya remarked on this peculiarity of fable poetry, noting that the fable, "in order not to dwell too long on the characterization of the personages, chooses those personages who reveal their nature by their name alone and serve as an understood concept. These characters are the animals." He then compares the fable figures with a game of chess: "In chess, each piece has a particular move: the knight moves in one way, the king and queen in other ways; this is known to everyone who plays the game."[3]

This fact is taken into consideration primarily by Aesop. Of course, the fox in Krylov's *Fox and the Grapes* and the wolf in his *Wolf and Lamb* behave just as in the fables of Aesop, Phaedrus, La Fontaine, and other fabulists. But each fabulist's individuality, and especially Krylov's, accounts for his altering the plot, as well as showing the characters in a different light. Pushkin's friend, Pyotr Pletnyov, aptly defined the animals in fables as "allegorical actors" representing man.[4] Krylov's lions, asses, bears, foxes, and eagles are not allegorical personifications, but the people themselves with their weaknesses and vices, vainglory, impudence, cunning, ingratitude, treachery, envy, cowardice, lies, and so on. They are as realistic as human characters, usually speak as expressively, and perform little comedies and dramas which reveal vices and virtues.

Belinsky wrote:

The very personifications in the fables ought to be lively, poetic figures. Thus every animal in Krylov's fables has his individual character—the mischievous monkey, whether it plays in a quartet, diligently shifts a block, or tries on spectacles in order to be able to read; the fox is ubiquitously cunning, evasive, and unscrupulous, indeed, more like a man than a fox "with feathers on its snout"; the clumsy bear is always good-natured, honest, slow-moving, and strong; the lion is menacingly powerful and awe-inspiring. The collision of these beings invariably gives rise to a little drama wherein each one exists in its own right, but forms a single integral whole with the others. This is achieved by intensive characterization, typification, and artistry in those fables whose characters include the fat tax-farmer who does not know how to escape the tedium of his money and the poor cobbler who is nonetheless happy with his fate; the philosophizing, ignorant cook who goes without cucumbers because of his superfluous learning; the peasant politicians and so on. Now this is real comedy![5]

This "animal masquerade" helps intensify the satirical humor of the fables by contributing a grotesque pointedness. Animals endowed with human characteristics emphasize the absurdities of the situations, and Krylov's natural attitude toward their escapades makes their behavior and conversations funnier still.

II *Humor in the Fable*

On the subject of humor in the fable, Georg W. F. Hegel defined its nature and peculiarity: "The humor is contained in the very lightness where the joke is combined, as it is, with extremely serious matters. This helps obtain a very graphic depiction of human baseness through depicting situations and proceedings in the animal kingdom."[6] For Hegel the most important aspect of a fable was its satirical tendency, and he saw the portrayal of the animals as a caricature of human relations.

The fabulous animals of Aesop and the *Panchatantra* were not intended for comic effect, but those of La Fontaine and especially Krylov were very funny indeed. Their behavior discloses human weaknesses and vices as if in a distorting mirror.

In *Two Dogs* the scene is conveyed in a dialogue between a

farmyard hound who does his guard duty honestly despite the
deprivation and the spoilt court favorite, Toy. The dogs' personalities at once reveal human characteristics:

> "Well, Toy dear, tell me how you fare
> Since Master took you in, to live with him up there?
> Out here we often starved, you've not forgotten how?
> Say, what's the job you're doing now?"
> " 'Twere wicked to complain," says Toy;
> "I'm sure I'm Master's only joy;
> I live in luxury and state;
> I eat and drink off silver plate,
> And play on Master's lap, and when that fancy's gone,
> The sofa and the floor are nice to roll upon."

And when the hound asks in amazement: "But how did you
on such good fortune fall,/ You, who are only weak and small?"
Toy replies, in a moment of confidence: "My job! That's good!
Say that again!"/ Cries little Toy, and sniggles up her jaws:/ "I
walk on my hind paws." (VII, 22)

This is an extremely expressive description of the idle syco-
phant, who, thanks to his servility to those in power has become
a favorite, while the honest laborer is condemned to hunger and
cold. Once again the author's concluding moral, "And many a
fortune had no other cause!/ The man could only walk on his
hind paws," is almost superfluous. The characters speak for themselves. Morals are always more convincing if they flow naturally
from the narrative than when they are appended as an abstract
conclusion.

We have noted more than once that the dramatic principle
often turns Krylov's fables into a dialogue between the characters.

The dramatic and scenic qualities particularly stand out in
The Soup of Master John. It actually begins with a dialogue
that reveals the characters' personality, and this is so true to
life that any thought of moral teaching does not enter the
reader's head:

> "Now do, old fellow, do!
> This dish was specially for you."

"No, my dear fellow, no: I'm simply stuffed." "No matter!
  There's room for just one little platter.
By gum, on soup like this, it's just a joy to sup!" (V, I)

It is as if we would have unwittingly eavesdropped on an argument. Master John is treating his neighbor, Master Tom, to fish soup. We see how excessively hospitable and insistent the host is and how obedient Master Tom is, afraid of offending his host. At the beginning of the fable Master John seems to be simply a cordial host, but when Master Tom says: "I've had three helpings now," and he answers affectionately: "What, counting every bite? Why, where's your appetite?" he becomes a tormenting despot. Master Tom is not in a position to refuse the host and keeps a grip on himself for fear of appearing impolite or ungrateful, although eating the soup is now a veritable torture for him: "You see from Thomas' face the perspiration pour;/ Perspire or not perspire, he takes one helping more."

This amusing duel between Master John and Master Tom ends with Tom running away, unable to put up with any more hospitality. The whole scene is based on brilliant dialogue and fine nuances in the speech of the participants. The very first lines in which John addresses Thomas are honey-toned and ingratiating. They convey the host's pride, his respect for the guest, and simple-hearted insistence. But they are also importunate and admit of no refusal:

"Now do, old friend! Just help me out!
  Here's perch, and here's some tripe, and here's a piece of trout.
    Just half a helping, do!
  You ask him, wife; perhaps he will for you."

How enticingly Master John enumerates the gastronomical qualities of the soup! His words bristle with diminutive suffixes. The contrast makes the concluding lines of the fable seem even more laconic when Thomas runs away:

But here, in sheer dismay,
  Though fond enough of soup, old Tom gets up straightway;
    Hat, belt and stick
    He gathers quick
  And runs for home with might and main,
And Master John won't see that friend again.

One of Krylov's most brilliant fables is *The Liar*. The plot is taken from Gellert's fable, *Peasant and his Son,* which was elaborated in Russian by Sumarokov in his fable *Boaster*. Krylov's fable, however, is so original that it is difficult to put it in the same category as its predecessors. It contains the true-to-life and at the same time typical portrait of a liar, the germ of Khlestakov in Gogol's comedy *The Inspector-General.* Apart from being a liar, the hero is also an inveterate cosmopolitan, frivolous, and a coward. Through his cowardice he exposes himself as a liar. The liar's psychology is revealed through his actions, whether he is confidently relating cock-and-bull stories or, meeting with disbelief, attempting to play them down. This is all conveyed in a lively, witty dialogue, or rather, monologue of the Liar himself, told with various intonations and a great wealth of language. The entire fable, from the very first lines, is permeated by the author's caustic irony.

Krylov's *Liar* is "A certain nobleman—most probably a prince," that is, a man from the privileged classes who has been abroad. He paints a rosy picture to his friends of fantastic wonders and speaks with contempt of his native land:

> Now, what's this country worth?
> Too hot, too cold, and all along
> This sun of yours is always wrong;
> First the snows of winter hide him,
> And then he shines so bright, you can't abide him.
> Well, there's a little heaven on earth;
> Bright thoughts its memory still excites. (II, 13)

Like Gogol's Khlestakov, the liar is carried away by his own lies: he tells of a cucumber which he saw in Rome that was as big as a mountain. But Krylov's liar is also a coward. His friend answers his bragging by warning him about the perfidious nature of the bridge over the river they have to cross:

> ... though simple it may seem
> It's quite of a peculiar class:
> There's not a liar here will dare that bridge to pass;
> Perhaps half-way across he'll stumble;
> Then sure as ever, off he'll tumble.

As soon as he hears these words, Krylov's liar lowers his tone, admits that the cucumber that he claims he saw was not as big as a mountain, but more like a house and, in fact, a house into which two persons would fit with difficulty, and moreover, they could not stand or sit in it.

Thus we see that the behavior of the characters in Krylov's fables is not stereotyped, but peculiar to human nature. It was by creating these typical and memorable characters that Krylov became the forerunner of the great Russian Realist writers of the nineteenth century.

III   *Details from Everyday Life*

We should also value the accurate background of Krylov's fables. The events he describes take place under specific conditions peculiar to Russian life which he depicts in a few graphic strokes. In *The Liar*, for example, the liar's friend describes the miraculous bridge and gives a few instances of accidents which allegedly occurred to representatives of those professions considered at that time to include the greatest number of liars:

> No stranger than our bridge, a hundred yards ahead;
>> For safe across it lets no liar go.'
>>> Why, just this spring, you know,
>>> From off that bridge there fell,
>>> As all the town could tell,
>> Two journalists, one tailor, too;   (II, 13)

This is a mischievous joke on Krylov's part: the friend only wants to frighten the liar, but the backlash of this detail also hit its mark, for journalists, such as the reactionary Bulgarin and Grech, used to resort quite often to lies in their search for sensationalism.

Krylov's fables were the first literary works to give the reader an unvarnished picture of the life of the Russian peasant, bureaucrat, and landowner. Many of his fables are miniature accounts of everyday life, charming for their originality and wealth of detail. They anticipated the accurate sketches of everyday life made by the Russian writers of the Natural School in

the 1840's. Let us consider by way of example one of Krylov's
later fables, *Shepherd Sandy*:

> In Shepherd Sandy's flock—he kept the master's sheep—
>> The sheep were getting less and less;
>>> So great was his distress,
> It made this fine young fellow weep;
> He oft was noticed crying, and let out:
>> "Friends, there's a dreadful wolf about!
>> He's started dragging all my sheep away,
>>> And tears the pretty dears to pieces."
>>> "And that is no surprise," they say;
>>> "With wolves about, no sheep at peace is."
>>> They're all agog, that wolf to spy.
> But how does Sandy's kitchen range supply
> Now loin of lamb with groats, now soup with mutton bone?
>> He'd been a cook, but falling in disgrace,
>> Was sent to mind the flock at master's country place
>> And so his cookery was rather like our own.
>> All hunt to catch the wolf; the wolf is blamed all round;
>> They search the forest through, but ne'er a wolf is found!
>> My friends, you waste your pains; the wolf idea came handy:
>>> Who eats the sheep? Why, Sandy.   (IX, I)

The basis of this fable is a plot taken from Russian life, a folk
proverb: "The talk is only about the wolf, but the sheep are
filched by Savva." In addition, the everyday life of the landed
gentry is accurately depicted in a thumbnail sketch. Sandy is
a serf lad whom the landlord took away from his village to his
own house in town so he could have him as a personal servant.
The lad committed some kind of an offense in town, was sent
back to the village as a punishment, and was demoted from
cook to shepherd. But Sandy is now used to town life and to his
master's good food. So, not only did he not turn over a new
leaf, but turned thief in order to maintain his style of eating
well. Thus we see that Krylov was able to show a bright peasant
lad who fools the village with his complaints about an innocent and non-existent wolf. The fable contains not merely a
moral about the swindler who covers up his track, but also a
picture of country life. The fabulist does not particularly hold

Sandy guilty for his cunning; in fact, he rather likes this clever peasant boy.

Let us consider yet another fable, *Squirrel on His Wheel.* The scene is painted with extreme precision:

> On Sunday at the Hall,
> Beneath a window, on the ground,
> The country folk were staring one and all,
> To see a squirrel on his wheel go round; (IX, 2)

Krylov gives us an expressive, though compressed, picture of a festive occasion in the country, drawn from real life. Even the dialogue which follows between the Thrush and Squirrel reads like a real dialogue:

> Upon a birch-tree near a thrush was watching too.
> He ran so fast, his paws went whirling like the wind,
> His fluffy tail spread out behind
> "Now come," says Thrush, "old fellow, tell us do,
> What you are after? Won't you say?"
> "Good friend, I'm hard at work all day;
> I'm special courier to a Minister of State;
> To eat, or drink, or take my breath,
> I have no time, I'm run to death!"
> And Squirrel starts again at yet a faster rate.
> Says Thrush, as he goes off: "We see, you can't keep still;
> And yet, you never leave that window-sill."

The moral of the fable is particularly appropriate: the Squirrel represents a smart dealer who is constantly engaged in something, hurrying lest he let a profit slip by, but in reality, making no progress:

> Just watch the busy fool, who thinks he's someone great!
> Folks stare; he fusses round, and can't be quieted;
> He twists and wriggles like an eel.
> And yet he never gets a yard ahead
> Like Squirrel on his wheel.

The humor and the moral are achieved by a complete parallelism between the Squirrel's actions on the wheel and the "busy fool," for they are both convinced that their feverish activity

is indisputably important, whereas an outsider can easily see
the futility of their ceaseless running around the wheel.

Thus, Krylov's fable personages are taken from real life and
represent particular types, and are not purely allegorical abstractions. Unlike La Fontaine's fables, it is not the moral, but
the realistic casing—the social and psychological characterization—which are important. This explains why the moral is
pushed into the background by pictures and scenes of real life
painted in the bright colors of everyday life. At the same time,
Krylov is not a portrayer of genre scenes. The detailed depiction
of everyday life was by no means the most important aspect of
his fables, as it was with his numerous imitators, among them
Izmaylov and Sukhanov. Krylov injected important principles
and ideas into his fables, and created satire having a broad
social application.

IV   *The Characters*

The characters in Krylov's fables frequently broke with their
traditional roles in fables. In *Crow and Fox*, for example, the
fox, in conformity with tradition, is the bearer of negative
qualities, namely flattery and untruthfulness. By means of
flattery he makes the crow lose the cheese she was holding in
her beak. At the beginning of the fable Krylov even gives the
following warning:

> How often have they told us, please,
> And always to no use—that flattery's mean and base?
> The flatterer in our hearts will always find a place. (I, I)

In spite of this warning, the fox's character—as revealed in the
fable—is not a disgraceful one by any means. Krylov's fox is
not a mere allegorical representation of the flatterer. He is clever,
resourceful, and eloquent. He deftly mocks the vain crow who
is not only susceptible to flattery, but is stupid and pompous,
and does not, therefore, evoke any sympathy on the part of the
reader. The fox does not flatter because he has to, as though it is
against his will, but in order to make fun of the crow.

When Krylov censures hypocisy, he does not adopt the position of the rhetorician like the cook in the fable *Cat and Cook*. He resorts to irony and lashes the hypocrite fiercely for his fawning and ostentatious loyalty (*Pop-a-Pop*).

Thus, in the biting fable *The Village Band*, Krylov does not make any accusations, but simply draws a picture of loyal decency which upon examination turns out to be a humbug. The fable tells how a music lover wanted to boast to his neighbor about his choir, and invited the neighbor to hear his band. The result, however, was lamentable:

> The Village Band struck up—too sharp, too flat, no matter;
> They made the roof resound.
> Jones felt his ears were splitting with this clatter,
> His head went whirling round.   (I, 3)

Most significant is the music lover's reaction to his guest's surprise: "Your village band . . . is mercilessly out of tune."

> "Well, yes," said Smith, with feeling in his tone,
> "I'm bound to own,
> They're not musicians highly skilled;
> But all are members of the Parish Guild,
> And all have signed the pledge."

But the sobriety of the singers is no evidence of their good singing and musical gifts. The master's fondness for his sober but giftless singers is shown with scathing irony. This is no allegory, it is an incident taken from life. Nonetheless, the fable can be applied generally to stigmatize hypocritical loyalty. This is why it does not age. But, Krylov could not keep from adding a personal, concluding remark: "But as for me, I'd let them drink all day/ If only they could play."

The fable is a genre which does not allow for any verbosity or lack of clarity. It is a short story in verse, condensed to the limit. That is why its characters must have traits as clearly defined as can be, and this is how they are in Krylov's fables. In the fable *The Hare a-Hunting*, the braggart hare manages to get a share—though inconsiderable—of the bear which is being divided up, thanks to his impudence and ability to amuse his mighty partners. Nobody had taken any notice of the hare when he announced: "Who was it scared him from the forest? I."

This kind of boastfulness, though no one's sense abusing,
Seemed so exceedingly amusing,
A tuft of Bruin's ear was given him in the end.   (II, 15)

The hare is not simply a braggart. He is resourceful, impudent, and cleverly takes stock of the situation. All this is conveyed in a tiny scene of nineteen lines.

The most successful portrayals of characters, however, are those of humans, because Krylov is not then tied to the animal characters imposed by tradition. The fable *Cat and Cook*, for example, regardless of its historical significance (it was written in connection with events immediately preceding the War of 1812), creates a typical image of the lover of idleness and rhetoric, who finds his inspiration in wine. The fable is spattered with colorful details: the Cook is both a "lettered man" and a "good soul," although Krylov adds ironically that he "didn't want to miss poor Andrew's funeral party" and that is why he stopped by at the tavern. At the same time, the Cook is not simply a drunkard and given to didactic admonitions, but a pompous and limited phrase-monger, who does not notice the sterility of his speeches, intoxicated as he is by his own eloquence. This can all be gathered from his graphic description.

Krylov's characters are true representatives of diverse sections of society, such as the court élite (*A Great Lord* and *Statesman and Thinker*), the moneyed élite (*Rich Man and Cobbler* and *The Bag*), the judiciary (*Pike* and *Peasant and Sheep*), and the peasantry (*Two Countrymen* and *Old Mat and his Man*).

Alongside these fables which emphasize social wrongs, Krylov wrote fables the main task of which was to point out a moral by depicting weaknesses and imperfections common to all mankind—*The Liar, The Miser, Pig under the Oak*. But in these cases, too, the characters are living beings.

V   *The Conclusions of Fables*

Plot development is one of the most important features of Krylov's fables. It contains the movement of the fable and the interrelation of its characters. It is the means whereby the moral or "soul" of the fable is revealed.

Whether the fable begins with a straight lead-in to the action or with the characters' dialogue or monologue, the plot develops in such a way that at the very end it undergoes a sharp change: a catastrophe takes place. The course of the action is unexpectedly cut short by a short phrase, witty retort, or joke which becomes the turning point of the fable.

This conclusion usually, though not always, occurs in the very last lines or line of the fable. It casts a new light on all that has gone on before, revealing the true meaning of it all. It does not, however, take the place of the author's moral which is found at the end or the beginning of the fable, though in many cases the author's opinion coincides with it, in which case there is no separate moral added to the fable.

In *Monkey and Mirror*, the conclusion of the fable is in the form of the bear's advice to the monkey who is grimacing in front of the mirror, although she herself has censured her friends for the very same thing. Not only does the conclusion disclose the moral of the fable, but it takes the place of a separate moral: "Instead of counting friend on friend,/ 'Twere best if to yourself you first of all attend!" (V, 8).

This conclusion usually completes the development of the plot by expressing the characters' reappraisal of their false understanding of reality. Occasionally it is a rejoinder by one of the characters expressing the author's own opinion. Such for instance is the Ass's reply in *The Elephant in Favour*: "I saw it at a glance;/ Without his nice long ears, he never stood a chance!" (V, 19)

Stupid though he is, the Ass—himself the owner of long ears—made his point: the Elephant really did not have anything else in his favor.

The conclusion does not, in principle, replace the author's moral which is usually separated from the narrative of the plot. *Ass and Rustic* tells of an ass whom a peasant hired to chase crows and sparrows from his garden. Despite the ass' good intentions in chasing the birds, he trampled all over the garden. The conclusion follows:

> So finding all his labour end in loss,
> The peasant on the Ass's back
> Repaid his loss with whack on whack. (VI, 11)

But Krylov did not consider that this took the place of the moral, and added at the end:

> I do not seek at all, the ass to justify!
> He's paid the penalty, and so he should, say I;
> But don't you think the man might ask himself for pardon
> For trusting to an ass to watch his kitchen garden?

The fable *The Strong Ant* is about a vainglorious ant whose strength was "quite enormous" and who was renowned in his ant hill for it. It went to his head and he decided to "show himself in town" "that there his strength might win renown." But, he fell on a cart full of hay and however hard he tried to attract attention to himself, he remained unnoticed:

> How is it, no one pays the notice that they owe me
> For all the feats that I display?
> Now if you come our way,
> I fancy all our anthill know me. (VI, 14)

This arrogant tirade of the ant, totally exposes his conceit and self-assurance. Krylov, however, adds the author's conclusion to generalize the incident:

> And that's the way
> The clever fool mistakes;
> He thinks the world re-echoes with his name
> And wakes,
> To find his anthill's bounds the limit of his fame.

Krylov usually wrote his fables as a response to some topical event or situation, but only if the event or situation was typical and instructive so that the fable could be of really general significance and be remembered for generations. This starting point for the fable is usually forgotten, unless it is dug up by some pedantic commentator whose labor-consuming research reveals the historical source of the fable. The fable quickly loses contact with the actual fact which gave rise to its origin, and acquires the generality which is the secret of its long life.

VI *The Character of the Narrator*

A very important element in Krylov's fables is the character of the narrator, the fabulist himself. The fables are told in the first person, which is, indeed, one of the definitions of its literary structure. Krylov has firmly secured for himself the popular nickname of "Dedushka Krylov" ("Grandpa Krylov"), which is a reference both to the popular wisdom of his fables and to the very character of the worldly-wise narrator. Although the fabulist does not usually intervene in the action of the fable directly, his presence is nonetheless felt behind the characters' dialogues or the narrative, even though he speaks in the first person only in the moral which begins or ends the fable.

A good illustration of this point can be made with the fable *Wolf and Cuckoo*. It relates how a wolf complains to a cuckoo that everybody around him, whether people or dogs, "the same bad temper show." In his resentment, he decides to leave for an ideal country, the forests of Arcadia where

> "You talk of war—and none will understand.
> The men are mild as lambs, you know."

But the cuckoo asks the wolf mistrustfully:

> "But your teeth, and your nice character
> —You take them too, or leave them here?"

to which the idealist Wolf answers: "What leave them? Never fear!" And when the Cuckoo hears this answer, she replies: "Then mark my words, my friend! You stand to lose your fur!" (II, 17)

This dialogue is completed by the direct participation of the author:

> The lower be your mind,
> The more to criticise in other folks you find!
> For such there's none that's good, where'er his eye may fall;
> Himself is first to quarrel with them all.

Here one feels particularly strongly the discrepancy between the conversational style of the dialogue and the literary style of the author's didactic conclusion. In other fables the moral is as lively as the unfolding of the plot and is virtually a second fable to shed light on the first. Such is the conclusion of *Crow*. This fable is written on the basis of a plot from Aesop. It tells how a vainglorious crow adorned herself with peacock feathers and claimed that she was a peacock. But her vain boasting was soon exposed and she was plucked by the peacocks who did not take her for one of them. When she returned to her own kind, they refused to recognize her, too. And so: "Poor thing! She'd ceased to be a crow,/ But was she peacock? Oh dear no!" (VII, 26).

The conclusion Krylov adds to this fable is not only written in typical Russian style, but switches the fable to the contemporary world.

> With just a little tale my fable I will match.
> A pleasant thought occurred to grocer's daughter, Flo.
>   Thought she: "I fancy I'm a catch;
>   Full fifty thousand pounds a pretty sum!"
>   They married honest Flo to Lord Tom Thumb.
> And what? Her husband's friends all teased her to satiety;
> "Her father was in trade! The height of impropriety!"
> Her sisters called her snob, for joining high society.
>   So there she was, poor, honest Flo,
>   No peacock and no crow.

These are the fabulist's own words to the reader, meant as an explanation of the allegorical meaning of the fable.

Krylov's contemporaries considered that one of the fable's most important characteristics was the naïveté of the fable teller. Izmaylov, for example, the author of the treatise "On the Fabulist's Tale," quotes the French literary critic Marmontel on La Fontaine:

We find in him not a poet who indulges in the delights of the imagination, nor a wit whose aim is to entertain us with his tale, but a first-hand witness of an event who tries to set it before us in such a lively way that we should feel we saw it ourselves and for this purpose uses all his learning, eloquence, philosophy, politics, all his imagination, memory, and sensitivity. These efforts, this totally convincing tone with which La Fontaine speaks of imaginery beings and trifles as if they were real and important events: the part he takes in the *Hare and the Swallow,* makes us exclaim, almost all the time we are listening to him, "Oh the simpleton!" (*le bonhomme*). That is what he was called in society and his character was transmitted to his fables.[7]

This characterization applies in full measure to Krylov, too. The naïve tone of the tale was essential to his fables; it enhanced the humor of the situations and created the impression that the narrator was directly involved in the events, for behind the action of each fable and the behavior of its characters is felt the presence of the author who comments on the events he has witnessed and explains the true significance of what has happened. Krylov usually writes in the first person only at the beginning or in the moral at the end. But his presence colors the whole account with its mischievous irony and wise appraisal:

> *But as for me,* I'd let them drink all day
>   If only they could play.
>   (*The Village Band,* I, 3)

> And cooks there are to whom *I'd say,*
> "Write up upon your kitchen wall:—
> By Order: Waste no words at all,
>   For cats aren't taught that way!"
>   (*Cat and Cook,* III, 8)

The opinion of the author is not only important in itself for the conclusion he makes from the fable, but also for its satirical sense; it is the light in which the events related in the fable must be looked at.

Even when Krylov does not include a moral in the first person, the author's attitude to the events can be gathered from the body of the fable. *Gardener and Wiseacre* contrasts practical knowledge to abstract theorizing. It shows the sober and practical gardener who looks after his garden sensibly and is rewarded a hundredfold for his pains. Opposed to this is the "wiseacre" who does not know the practice of gardening, but does everything according to theories from books and as a result "gets no gherkins" while the gardener brings in a rich harvest.

The very narrative of this fable is done with an ironical tone directed at the "wiseacre":

> Our scholar to his study hies;
> He reads, collates and verifies;
> He digs in books, he digs in furrows,
> Researches, ramifies and burrows. (III, 10)

Despite the objectivity of this account, the author's attitude is skeptical toward the wiseacre's diligence. That is why the concluding lines of the fable merge with the tone of the narrative without separating into a special moral:

> The gardener's crop comes up; he takes it in to town,
> And gets his profit, money down!
> But wise man Perkins
> Has got no gherkins!

Much more complicated is the speech construction of the fable *Fortune and the Beggar,* which has no moral either. This is a fable about human greed, the invariable discontent with one's estate, and the inability to stop hoarding wealth. The tale is told in the third person, which allows for an objective exposition of events.

> With wallet patched and worn, his weary footsteps trailing,
> A beggar passed a house, and, gazing upward yonder
> And at his own privations railing,
> Could not repress his wonder
> That some can make their homes as gorgeous as they please,
> And wallow deep in wealth and luxury and ease
> And yet, howe'er their pockets they may stuff,
> Have ne'er enough. (V, 22)

Then follows a monologue of the beggar's thoughts, also in the third person:

> For instance, now, the man who used to own that mansion
> Took up some lucky trade affair
> Which grew to vast expansion.
> Instead of stopping there
> And finishing his days without a single care,
> His business sold, with plenty and to spare,
> He launched at turn of spring full many a gallant prow;
> He hoped for piles of gold:—his ships are at the bottom;
> The treasures they brought, the hungry deep has got 'em;

At last Fortune appears before the beggar and says to him:

"Of how to help you, friend, it's long that I've reflected;
This heap of sovereigns I've collected;
Put out your knapsack! There!
I'll fill it to the top;
But here my favors stop;
Each sovereign as it falls is pure and solid gold;
But all the shining coins your knapsack cannot hold
Will turn to rubbish as they drop." (V, 22)

The delighted beggar holds out his knapsack, but greed over-powers him, and although the wallet is overflowing, he still demands more and more gold. Then comes the culmination of the fable conveyed in an energetic, fast-moving dialogue:

"Enough?" "Oh no, not yet!" "It's splitting!" "Never mind!"
"You're rich as Croesus now!" "Please, please, a little more,
One handful! Room I'll find!"

In the end the pouch bursts and the treasure disappears.

The moral of the fable is revealed by means of the plot and is summed up in an objective statement by the author: "Our beggar-man remains a beggar, as at first."

On many occasions the fabulist starts, as it were, an argument with the reader, interrupting his narrative with addresses to him. Thus, at the beginning of the fable *Peasant and Dog*, Krylov himself expresses amazement at the absurdity of what is going on in his tale:

A peasant in a very prosperous way
With house and farm, once took into his pay
A dog—to guard the court from roving beggar's tread,
To bake the bread,
To water and to trim the garden every day.
"Good Lord! What utter trash he writes!"
The indignant reader says: "There's not the least pretence
Of sense;
Allow, he watched the yard at nights;
But when did dogs bake bread, that anybody knows,
Or trim and water cabbage-rows?"
No, reader! My ideas are not so out of joint,
That I should say they did, but that is not the point.
That Rover took the job—the point is there! (IX, 6)

The position of the fabulist is clear from the very beginning: he looks upon the many duties undertaken by the dog with skepticism. Krylov lifts the boundary between the fable itself and the moral admonition, and abandons the objective account of the events in the third person. But the author's encroachment on the fable happens comparatively rarely with Krylov.

In a number of fables Krylov endows the image of the author with his own personal autobiographical traits. In the introduction to the fable *The Young Roach,* for instance, he speaks about himself and justifies this in his own way:

> That's only just a baby fable:
> The real one's coming after it.
> That's just the moral of my meditations.
> There! In your eyes I now see new preoccupations;
> At first—too short and now, unless I'm wrong,
> You fear it will be long.
> Well, what is there to do, dear friend? Have patience!
> That's what I fear myself!
> But how can it be helped? I'll soon be on the shelf.
> The autumn rain goes pitter-patter;
> Old folks are oft inclined to chatter . . . (VII, 5)

Krylov wrote his fables as the bearer of national wisdom and the judge of human foibles and vices. Or, as Academician Y. Grot wrote:

Krylov the man could, of course, have his faults in his personal life; but the person who appears in his fables is a lofty sage full of rules of honor and virtue, a persecutor of all types of lies and baseness, a defender of science and thought against ignorance and stupidity, and, finally, the mentor of his contemporaries and of posterity.

Grot is correct in adding: "His fables are significant not as fables, but as works which artistically embody the intelligence and wisdom of experience of all the people."[8]

That is why the moral verdicts passed in the didactic "tail-piece"—the author's conclusion—acquire the force of a popular saying and the power of an indisputable experience of the community. Thus, the fable *Froggy and Jupiter* which tells of the frog who asked Jupiter to flood the earth to the level of a mountain on which she had selected a "cozy nook among the broken ground" for herself, is accompanied by a moral censuring egoism:

> And many men I've seen, so mean in character
> That self becomes the worst of crazes:
> If they can have what they prefer,
> Then all the world can go to blazes! (V, 23)

The censure of private interest contrasted to the advocacy of "the common good" is precisely what constitutes popular wisdom. In the fable *Swan, Pike and Crab,* Krylov attacks lack of cooperation:

> When partners can't agree,
> Their business fares disastrously;
> With worry all the while, they get no further on. (IV, 5)

These verdicts of the author in verse easily turn into proverbs. The last line of the introduction to the fable *Hermit and Bear* has long been a proverb:

> Though help in time of need is precious, as we know,
> Not every one such timely help can lend;
> Heaven save you from a foolish friend;
> *The too officious fool is worse than any foe.* (IV, 11)

In such introductions the author is not being allegorical, but directly states his opinion, often underlining it with the use of the first person:

> *You ask me what I think?* The advice is good, *I grant;*
> Yet sail without a wind, you generally can't.
> (*The Swimmer and the Sea,* VI, 10)

> *I do not seek* at all, the ass to justify!
> He's paid the penalty, and so he should, *say I;*
> But don't you think the man might ask himself for pardon,
> For trusting to an ass to watch his kitchen garden?
> (*Ass and Rustic,* VI, 11)

Krylov relates the feats of the brave ant (*The Strong Ant*) in the grave manner of a historian and, at the same time, with

humor. The humor arises from the incongruity of the grand style
and the insignificant "exploits" of the self-important ant:

Now once there was an ant whose strength was quite enormous;
Since first the world began, his fellow ne'er was born;
He even—so with truth the chronicles inform us—
Could pick you up with ease two grains of barley-corn.
Then as to bravery, such pluck was never known;
    A worm he wouldn't look at twice,
        But nipped it like a vice,
And often would attack a spider all alone.   (VI, 14)

This is an example of the "merry mischievousness" that Pushkin spoke about, raving about the bold simplicity of Krylov's
imagery: "and often would attack a spider all alone." Pushkin
considered that as far as "boldness of invention" went, this metaphor was on a level with the imagery of such geniuses of world
literature as Milton and Molière.[9]

The fables of Aesop, Phaedrus, and Lessing tell us virtually
nothing of the authors' attitudes. The action in the fables is
related without their evaluation. In Krylov's fables, on the other
hand, one always feels the author's irony, sympathy, and argu-
mentative spirit. This is felt in the intonation, the choice of
epithets, and in the very pointedness of the caricatures. This
is what made him so popular and won him the nickname "Grandpa Krylov."

VII   "Merry Mischievousness"

"The merry mischievousness of Krylov" is the distinguishing
feature of his fables, said Pushkin. This "mischievousness" is
found in the undertone of irony, the caustic humor, and the
resourcefulness of the fabulist, who gives the appearance of
telling a story seriously, but who, in fact, is making fun of his
characters. Irony is the most important satirical weapon of the
fabulist; it is the prevailing tone of his fables.

The literary critic, Professor A. Nikitenko, a contemporary of
Krylov noted:

This is tranquil, mischievous, and, at the same time, good-natured
irony in which a deep and true understanding of things shines forth

from behind the ignorance claimed by it and the objective attitude to the question. . . . His irony took the form of the spirit of the people and received its particular physiognomy from it.[10]

The apparent naïveté of the narration which belies the author's deep and sober understanding of the world is the essence of the fabulist's irony. In *Mike among the Hives,* the bear, who becomes the hives' guardian, is far from being a funny character. Bit by bit he conveys all the honey to his lair, and his punishment is to be condemned to lie in his lair for a whole year. He gladly acquiesces to the penalty: " 'Tis nice inside his den to lie; He sucks his paw for hours together; No worse than waiting by the sea for weather!" This is all told in a simple and earnest tone, as if the narrator would believe in the justice of the court and the purposefulness of such a sentence, when he is, in fact, mocking the entire judicial procedure and the "punishment."

In *Monkey and Mirror* the source of the humor is in the monkey's imitation of humans, when she behaves like a woman of the world and, at the same time, is sincerely horrified upon catching sight of herself in the mirror.

> "Observe that awful phiz,
> The wrinkles of the brow, the strange grimaces there!
> I'd hang myself in sheer despair
> If I possessed a snout the slightest bit like this!" (V, 8)

In *Dogs' Friendship* the narrative begins in a strictly serious, neutral manner:

> Once Bob and Rover lay
> Outside the kitchen wall, a-basking in the heat.

But very soon an unexpectedly mocking tone insinuates itself:

> Though at the gateway of the yard
> They might with greater pomp have kept their guard.

Then follows a frankly ironic explanation of why the dogs were lazing in the kitchen instead of being on guard duty at the gates:

> Yet as they'd had their fill of meat—
> And well-behaving dogs by day

> Don't bark at those who pass their way,—
> The pair began to chat, and talked and talked away
> Of every mortal thing—the work they had to do,
> Of evil and of good, and last, of friendship too. (II, 5)

The dogs' long discourses on friendship are a parody of the sentimental style of Karamzin, who was Krylov's contemporary:

> Said Rover, "What could fortune happier send
> Than all your life to live with tried and trusted friend,
> To help each other out if trouble should arise,
> To sleep, to eat beside your brother,
> To fight like heroes for each other,
> To look with fondness in your comrade's eyes,
> To see that not one wasted chance went by
> To amuse your friend, to make his hours more bright.

The clichéd language of the Sentimentalists ("tried and trusted friend," "bright hours") lends a deliberately bookish and artificially sentimental character to the dogs' conversation. They are lying in the sun and their feelings for one another seem to have mellowed in its heat. But it only takes the cook to throw a bone out of the kitchen window for all their tenderness and oaths of eternal friendship to disappear into thin air:

> And see! the new-made friends are on it like a flash!
> Accord, agreement melt like wax.
> Orestes, Pylades, they bite, they tear, they gnash;
> They fill the air with clumps of wool . . .

This is the voice of the narrator again, this time giving the unvarnished truth about the worth of "dogs' friendship." The comic effect is enhanced by the fact that the sentimental sighs are emitted—and the beautiful, florid conversation about love and friendship is conducted—by dogs.

As he relates, or rather allows the characters to unfold the story of "the dogs' friendship," Krylov makes his appearance in the moral "tail-piece," not as the story-telling observer, but as a wise judge of human ways:

> Of friendship such as this the world is full;
> In fact, 'twould seem of friends there's scarce another kind;

Describe one pair of them, and all the rest you cover;
To hear them talk, you'd say they had one heart and mind;
Then throw them down a bone, and there's your dogs all over.

This stylistic variety, the alternation of voices with their different tones is a distinguishing feature of Krylov's fables. He avoids the monotony of the didactic manner by having several characters relate his fables.

The fable *The Ass* begins with the same mischievous tone ("The day when Jupiter first peopled all the earth"). The author makes no secret of his ironical attitude to the trouble the conceited ass goes to when he asks Zeus to make him at least as big as the calf:

Next day again
The ass took up the old refrain;
And this at last became so tiring,
Thought Zeus: "Oh let him have whatever he's desiring;
I'll set his mind at ease."   (I, 16)

This disrespectful tone towards the ass is kept up throughout the fable and leads up to the final judgement: "For sheer stupidity his name has come to pass:/ And all put burdens on his back."

Belinsky gave the following comprehensive description of Krylov's sense of irony:

In his fables he exhaustively and perfectly expressed a whole side of the Russian spirit: his fables faithfully mirror the Russian practical sense with its apparent sluggishness and also its sharp biting edge which can occasionally be painful; with its gumption, keen wit, and good-natured sarcastic mockery; with its innately sound way of looking at things and with the ability to express itself briefly, clearly, and at the same time artistically.[11]

VIII   *Rhythm, Intonation, and Rhyme*

Krylov imbued the lines of his fables with astonishing expressiveness. It seems as if their rhythm, intonation, and very sound convey the events related in the fable. He broke the rules of classical rhetoric to bring them closer to the spoken language. Gogol wrote on the subject:

Nor can one fathom his verse. There is no way of describing it: is it resounding? is it light? is it heavy? It is sonorous when the pace of the plot is fast, grows stronger where the thought consolidates, and becomes suddenly light where it gives place to the trivial chatter of a fool. His language is submissive and obedient to his thought, and flies like the wind, whether in a long, six-foot line or in the rapid one-footer; its very spirituality lies palpably in the calculated number of syllables in each line.[12]

Every line of the fables is made up of words each of which is prominent both for its intonation and for its rhythm; this gives them the energetic intonation of colloquial speech, and the effect is surprisingly expressive. Krylov based his fables on the free rhythmical flow of the line of poetry. All fables, and especially Krylov's, keep close to spoken speech and intonation. Krylov's verses are based on the structure of colloquial Russian speech. According to L. Timofeev, "speech verse" is based not on musical principles, but "only on the elements of language which lend the speech a mood which is purely personal and attain it only by means of language."[13] This "speech verse" had been anticipated in Russia by the traveling players whose facetious verses and burlesque shows laid the foundation of the verse which makes up Sumarokov's parables.

The line of poetry in Krylov's fables has a natural and conversational ring which determines the rhythmical pattern of the line.

In the fable *Bullfinch and Pigeon* this rhythmical pattern brings out the emotional, sincere tone of the speech. The pigeon's speech goes like this:

> "What, in broad daylight! Fancy at your age,
> > That you get caught!
> They don't catch me, though, I engage!
> They'll find that I am far too bright!" (V, 3)

> *Ne stýdno ľ,—govorít—spreď béla dnyá*
> > *Popásya!*
> *Ne provelí by tak menyá:*
> *Za éto ya rucháyus' smélo.*

The intonational, spoken line is distinguished by a different number of feet. In the fable's rhythmical structure the two-foot lines (and even more so the one-foot lines) are particularly expressive and are marked by their energetic intonation:

> Upon the passage floor,
> Half hidden by the door,
> An empty bag there lay;

> V *prikhózhey na polú,*
> V *uglú,*
> *Pustóy meshók valyálsya.*

The isolation of the phrase "half hidden by the door" in a separate line heightens the impression of the uselessness and abandonment of the old sack. Or take the following lines in the same fable (*The Bag*):

> Who thought an empty purse an ordinary evil
> Until they made their pile by sharing with the devil,
> With whom Lord Short-of-Cash, the Prince of Candle-Ends
> Are friends . . .

The separation of "are friends" in a line of its own completes the list of all those who were now the bag's friends and rounds it off with an ironic note.

The rhythmical pattern of the fables is particularly expressive, and vividly illustrates the meaning of the fable's tale. It is interesting to read what the Russian poet Zhukovsky had to say about Krylov's fable *Hermit and Bear*. He displayed a fine understanding of its intonational and rhythmical structure. He quoted these lines:

> Now look at Mike! He doesn't speak a word,
> But gathers up a stone of ponderous weight,
> Squats on his hinder paws,
> And scarce a breath he draws;
> "Hush, hush! You lively brute," thinks he, "I'll have you now,"
> And waiting till it lights above the hermit's brow,
> Smash, crash, he thumps the stone full on the sleeper's pate. (IV, 11)

Then wrote: "All these words: 'Mike, ponderous, stone, hinder paws, scarce a breath he draws, thinks, waiting till it lights' wonderfully depict slowness and carefulness; then after five long, heavy lines follows a half-line: 'smash, crash, he thumps the stone'—this is a flash of lightning, a sudden blow! It really creates a picture."[14]

We see that the rhythm and intonation of Krylov's line of poetry always set off and strengthen his meaning; they constantly interact with the plot and the development of the action of the fable. The urge to achieve expressiveness through intonation, a rhythmically unfettered line, also explains the rhyme system. Krylov does not go out of his way to write varied or unexpected rhymes. In his doggerel-like, conversational line of varying feet, the rhyme serves to link the lines closer together and also to add to the expressiveness of the sound. It does not emphasize the end of the line or the completion of a syntactic whole, but rests on the semantic and intonational articulation of the whole text. Hence, the constant repetition of rhyme and its contribution to the rhythm. Hence, too, the predomination of rhyming verbs.

Another factor which adds to the expressiveness of the fables is their sound. Apart from the imagery evoked by the words, Krylov also makes use of the expressiveness of sound itself, constantly having recourse to various types of sounds in order to set off the semantic structure of the fable.[15]

In his account of the pig that penetrated a squire's back-yard (*Pig*), Krylov creates a lifelike picture of the pig, conveying its smug snorting by means of onomatopoeia:

> Vsyo tol'ko lish navoz da sor;
> A, kazhetsya, uzh ne zhaleya ryla,
> Ya tam izryla
> Ves' zadniy dvor . . .

> (There's only rubbish and manure;
> And yet, I'm sure,
> I never spared my snout,
> And routed out
> The whole backyard.) (III, 16)

The repetition of the sounds *r*, *y* and *z* is particularly expressive here.

In the fable *The Plague of the Beasts*, Krylov makes use of onomatopoeia to convey the melancholy lowing of the ox, saturating his speech with such vowels as *y* and *u* in imitation of lowing:

> *I my*
> *Greshny. Tomu let pyat', kogda zimoy kormy*
> *Nam byli khudy,*
> *Na grekh menya lukavy natolknul;*
> *Ni ot kogo sebe nayti ne mogshy ssudy,*
> *Iz stoga u popa ya klok sentsa styanul.*

> (We too confess
> Our sins. Five years ago, what time our winter store
> Could give no more,
> The devil greatly urged me to transgress;
> And, after I had starved for nearly all the day,
> I plucked from parson's stack a little wisp of hay.) (II, 4)

Lobanov made the following remark about these lines: "Through the ox's speech we hear his lowing which seems so natural that his words cannot be changed for any other sound."[16] Thus, Krylov brings out the significance of sounds and enhances the emotionality of the language.

IX *The Expressiveness of the Language*

It was in Krylov's fables that the language of Russian literature (indeed, the language of verse!) was first discovered to have inexhaustible possibilities and limitless freedom from the artificial rules and regulations imposed by the Classicist theory of poetics.

The significance of the fables is not, by any means, confined to the genre. They represent a perfect fusion of poetic thought and imagery with their verbal expression—a fusion which determined the course of the Realist Movement. In the fables, the *language* became the real hero of the literary work, giving life to the fable characters and making them vivid and real.

The language of Krylov's fables is not the artificial, amusing doggerel of Sumarokov's fables, but truly popular, colorful, and descriptive, ignoring the Classicist ruling about the three styles, as advocated by Lomonosov in his *Rhetoric*. This division of the language into three styles—high, middle, and low—was largely based on the peculiarity of the formation of the Russian literary language which included not only Russian, but also Old Church Slavonic, the language of church literature. The high style was to be used for heroic themes and was composed mostly of Old Church Slavonic vocabulary with its abundance of hyperboles and declamatory tones. The low style was reserved for the fable, and favored the vulgar speech of peasants, coarse jokes, and a colloquial tone.

In his portrayal of scenes from peasant life, Krylov makes use of popular speech, but has little in common with crude burlesque. He makes poetry out of everyday language, and is sensitive to its shades of meaning, tenderness, and beauty. The simplicity of the works of the great fabulist was a result of their depth of content, the truly popular wisdom of his fables, and his supreme mastery of the language. He was the first to make use of the inexhaustible wealth of the common language and thereby expand the narrow bounds of the bookish style that prevailed before him.

"The poet and the sage became one in him," wrote Gogol about Krylov.

Everything he describes comes to life, starting with nature, captivating, menacing, and even dirty right up to the communication of the nuances in conversation which bring out spiritual qualities and make them live. Everything he says is said so aptly, and his understanding is so firm that it is impossible to determine what the character of his pen consists in. There is no way of categorizing his style. It is as if the subject has no verbal wrapping and presents itself to the reader without any outside help![17]

The individuality and expressiveness of Krylov's fables is determined by their kinship to the language of sayings, proverbs, and the satire and humor of folklore. Pyotr Vyazemsky, poet and contemporary of Krylov, made the following perceptive remark: "Dmitriev writes his fables; Krylov relates his."[18] Krylov fuses the language of the people and the language of literature, or rather, raises the former to the level of the latter. It is not surprising that Pushkin held Krylov in such high esteem for his "descriptive manner of expressing himself," and that he began his famous novel-in-verse *Evgeny Onegin* with a slightly paraphrased line from Krylov's fable *Ass and Rustic*: "A sire more honest ne'er existed" (from Krylov's "An ass more honest ne'er existed"). One might even say that this opening line served as a "tuning-fork" for the entire novel, fixing its Realistic character.

The academician V. Vinogradov produced a felicitous definition of the linguistic structure of Krylov's fables:

The language of Krylov's fables is full of verve and socially significant traits. It shows in abundance the various aspects of real Russian life with its typical everyday forms of expression, its dramatic conflicts, contradictions, struggles, sorrows, and joys. We see peasants, shepherds, millers, carters, merchants, tax-farmers, lords, clerks, hunters, poets, landowners, and high officials—in a word, Russians of different professions, classes, estates, and status; and we see them expressing themselves in typical language, though artistically elaborated. It is as if the hero of Krylov's fables were the language itself with its peculiarly national expressions, its interplay of vivid colors, its artistic potential, and its inherent way of thinking.[19]

The structure of the fables' language is based on the use of various styles subordinated to the integrity of the image of the author. The style may be conversational as in *The Sightseer*:

"Ah! glad to see you, Brown! Well, tell me where you've been?"
        "The new Museum, White,
        To spend an hour or two . . ." (IV, 15)

Or it may be colloquial, as in *Two Countrymen*:

"Good morning, Master Tom!"—"Good morning, Master Will!"
"Well, well, how wags the world with you, old chap?" (VII, 20)

In other cases it may be a conversational monologue by the author, told with mischievous irony in the restrained manner of a fairy tale, as in *Wolf and Fox*: "When Master Fox of food had had his fill one day/ And quite a tidy store had neatly stowed away . . ." (IV, 3).

The language of the fables is rich in proverbs, sayings, and popular phrases, all of which help to set a genuinely popular atmosphere. Phrases such as "Every family has something queer"

(*Elephant as Governor*), "They catch the eye—the tooth can't catch them" (*Fox and the Grapes*), "From frying-pan to fire" (*Mistress and Her Two Maids*), are typical examples.

Conversely, thanks to the strict economy of words, precision of the thought, vividness and rhythmical structure of the fables, many of their verses have been converted into proverbs and sayings.

The secret of Krylov's mastery of language was the ability to find the briefest way of expressing an idea which was at the same time poetic and graphic. Each line, each phrase is as concise as it could possibly be. Many of them were immediately adopted into the Russian language as proverbs: "This was a box that opened of itself" (*A Little Box*); "And God deliver us from critics half so blind" (*Ass and Nightingale*); "I'd let them drink all day if only they could play" (*The Village Band*); "Why should we cross the bridge. Why can't we find a ferry?" (*The Liar*); "The too officious fool is worse than any foe" (*Hermit and Bear*); "Then throw them down a bone and there's your dogs all over" (*Dogs' Friendship*); "The cat had polished off the meat" (*Cat and Cook*); "The elephant? I never noticed him" (*The Sightseer*); "Then change your seats, and fiddles too: Yet chamber music's not for you" (*A Quartet*). And there are countless other examples.

The astonishing thing about the language of the fables is that while being popular, it never descends to vulgarity, dialects, or crudity. It is a literary language that has absorbed the wealth of spoken speech. Consider the first lines of the fable, *A Comb*:

> To comb the fluffy head of pretty little Tom,
>   Mamma once bought a nice new comb.
> To Tom 'twas like a toy, he'd never let it be;
> And while he played at games or said his ABC,
>   He always combed his golden hair;
> As smooth and curly as a lambkin's fleece,
>   Like finest flax, so soft and fair,
> He combed it, and he combed, as if he could not cease. (VI, 3)

Krylov had no patience for ornamental or forced style. His language was precise and clear, and he did not hesitate to use expressions and words which did not sound acceptable to many of his contemporaries bred on the salon language of the Sentimentalists: "But strained so hard, she cracked and burst." Or: "The silly creature's head turns giddy with his praise."

When he worked on his fables, Krylov's main purpose was to make them simpler and more expressive. He found that the best way to achieve this was to make use of the language of the people. This can be seen in *Soup of Master John*, which has an abundance of affectionate and diminutive suffixes which endow the dialogue with an inimitable Russian atmosphere. How affectionate and yet at the same time full of dignity are the Russian addresses used in this fable, and the diminutives or the typically Russian expressions which are rendered as, "I'm simply stuffed," "No matter," "It's joy to sup," but which in fact cannot be exactly translated into any language.

X A Wealth of Styles

In some of Krylov's fables the use of diminutive suffixes lends a certain lyricism to them. In *The Kind Fox*, for example, the diminutives give the fable a sentimental air.

In *Two Countrymen*, however, the common speech gives a different flavor to the fable, it conveys the peasants' benightedness. They talk about the evils of drinking in mean, harsh words: "I'm punished for my sins," "And I go houseless still," "That's sorry kind of play," "With my friends I too had had a bout."

Krylov delighted in parodying the high style of Classicist poetry by transferring its lofty phraseology to the lower setting of everyday circumstances and common, colloquial language. He would often begin a fable with a solemn narrative in epic style which underlined the insignificance of the content:

The day when Jupiter first peopled all the earth,
(*The Ass*)

When out of Greece they drove the gods of ancient days . . .
(*Parnassus*)

Such "epic" openings ought to have lent weight to the event subsequently described, but in fact the development of the

fable was a comic contrast to the epic beginning. This can be
seen in *The Ass* in which the ass begs Jupiter to make him
taller, or in *Parnassus* where the asses gather on Mount Parnassus
and form their absurd choir there.

Another frequent device was, while maintaining an epic narrative tone, to substitute colloquial language for the lofty vocabulary: "Right into Squire's back-yard a pig his way had
found" (*Pig*, III, 16).

Krylov did not always keep to the same style; he would
change it in accordance with the theme of the fable, or with
the social setting described in it. The fables whose characters
are peasants in a village setting or animals (*Soup of Master
John, Two Countrymen, Peasant and Dog, Ass and Rustic, Shepherd Sandy, Wolf and Shepherds, Wolf and Cat* and many
others) are written in a rich, popular language, with an abundance of peasant idioms, vocabulary, and suffixes (affectionate
and diminutive) which are typical of popular speech. The fables
written in this style are his real masterpieces.

There are other fables about the professional classes such as
The Merchant, The Bag, and *Rich Man and Cobbler.* They
brim with the phraseology and terminology of merchants:

"Here, Tom, come here, my lad!
Wherever have you gone? I want you here at once.
        Your uncle's not done bad!
    Now just you trade like me, and then you'll be no dunce."
    To a nephew in his shop a merchant thus held forth;
        "You know that *worn-out piece* of Polish cloth,
'Twas here for all these years, and never *got a shake*." (VIII, 11)

Many of the fables are written in the lyrical style of the Sentimentalists, describing landscapes or lyrical scenes. The fable
The Brook, which the author himself particularly prized, began
in this style:

    A peasant by a brook poured forth a plaintive lay;
    He sang his heavy loss and his abiding woe;
        His favourite lamb not long ago,
        The neighbouring river swept away. (II, 9)

Further on there is the monologue of the brook which contrasts itself to the turbulent river:

> I'd count myself a pride to nature;
> I would not hurt a living creature!
> What care, what delicacy I would show
> Towards each hut, each shrub that I might chance to pass.

In the fables about animals, popular speech acquires the character of a folk tale. In the *Fox*, for example, which takes its plot from the famous fairy tale *Fox and Wolf*, the vocabulary and tone of the tale are preserved: "He let his brush's tip/ Inside the water dip,/ Of which the ice took hold." The fable is not stylized, but it is full of images and words which convey the atmosphere of the folk tale: "A tail so soft and downy, so fluffy and so reddy-browny," "He waits and waits; the tail gets faster still in prison."

In the fables *Peasant and Sheep* and *Pike*, the action reproduces the setting of court proceedings and Krylov uses the language of officials, parodying its bureaucratic bombast and clichés. A good example of this is to be found in the verdict passed by the judge (fox) in *Peasant and Sheep*:

> And here's the Fox's judgment, word for word:—
> "The pleas the sheep puts in, we find, are out of place;
>   Skill in removing every trace
>   Has always been a feature of the vicious;
> The evidence has proved that on the tenth of May
>   The sheep and fowls were never far away,
>   And fowls are most delicious;
>   All the conditions were propitious;
> Then, judging on my conscience, I decide,
>   She could not, as is shown,
>   Have left those fowls alone."
> The sheep's condemned to death. Be sentence straight applied!
> The meat remains in Court; the plaintiff takes the hide. (VII, 16)

This speech brilliantly exposes the cunning casuistry of the old judge—the lengthy and muddled exposition of his decision with its official phraseology and syntax overloaded with subordinate clauses.

This ability to write in different styles, using different vocabularies to match the characters of the fable is one of the distinguishing features of Krylov's genius.

The fables acquired their specific expressive character from their realistically precise and descriptive details, the vividness of the picture of everyday life, and the boldness of the similes. In *Froggy and Jupiter* the "domain" of the frog is described with painstaking thoroughness and at the same time apparent simplicity when it moves during springtime from the marsh to the mountain:

> Well up the neighbouring hill decided
> To make a move;
> There in a cosy nook among the broken ground,
> A little paradise she found. (V, 23)

Pushkin was correct in noting the boldness of Krylov's poetical imagination and the metaphorical vividness of his images. Consider the following lines from *Parnassus*:

> And such a discord rose from all the noisy throng,
> As if a train of wagons rolled along
> On twenty thousand wheels, and each one wanting grease. (I, 8)

Or the apt and graphic description of the ass with his bell:

> Our poor distinguished friend! He scarcely had moved a yard,
> The Order round his neck would tinkle hard; (VIII, 13)

Vinogradov remarked that "Krylov's imagery always rests on a witty, novel, and unexpected, but always thoroughly justified rapprochement of apparently incompatible meanings and concepts."[20] Krylov's metaphorical language is especially important; it forms the structural principle of his fables. The very title of, for example, *Sammy's Coat* in the context of the fable as a whole acquires an allegorical significance. Yet, the coat remains real—extremely worn, torn, and clumsily mended. The peculiarity of Krylov's images lies in their realism, in the ability to convey a "clear idea" and "poetical pictures," as Pushkin said.

The art of providing realistic details acquires a particular brilliance and significance in Krylov's fables. The details not only give a true ring to the description of everyday circumstances, but also help typify it.

The fable *Spider and Gout* is a good example:

> In rooms as splendid as can be,
> The Spider measured out the bounds of his domain;
> On wardrobe richly carved he builded,
> Or else along the cornice gilded
> Spreads everywhere his tangled skein . . . (V, 16)

The details, though sparing, paint a vivid picture of the magnificent setting which suits the spider's activities.

The fable *Geese* owes its realism and plausibility to its accurate details: "In long and trailing throng,/ The rustic brought his geese to town, to sell" (III, 15).

The epithets "long and trailing" are particularly telling. They add to the reality of the "throng" as if by divesting it of poetical conventionality.

Krylov's virtuoso-like mastery over the word never ceases to amaze. In Classicist poetry, the word was subject to a hierarchy of styles, and its inclusion in a text depended on what style it related to. In Krylov's works, on the other hand, the choice of words and images sprang from their use in real life and depended on the character, social status, and profession of the personage depicted.

Conclusion

THE main streams of Russian literature which determined its popular character, the national individuality of its forms, and its realism have their source in Krylov's fables. These streams are not separate parallel developments, but are mutually related and mutually benefiting aspects of one and the same process. Krylov's fables, appearing as they did in the first decade of the nineteenth century, boldly heralded a change in Russian literature from Classicism to Realism. This is because the fable is a satirical genre and hence has close connections with reality, with a specific social and political situation, and with an analysis of life in general. In addition, a tendency to typify and generalize is inherent in fables.

Krylov avoided not only the strictly allegorical and didactic manner of the ancient fable, but also the burlesque, "low" style characteristic of Russian Classicism and especially of Sumarokov. This style was not Realism, but was the result of looking upon life from above, which was not Krylov's way. His fables went beyond the hierarchical way of Classical thinking; they were not limited to mocking the "lowness" of everyday life. They contain a sober and generalized picture of contemporary Russian life, indicting not only universal vices and weaknesses, but the negative aspects of the tsarist régime in particular.

Krylov's fables were important for Russian literature of the nineteenth century in that they inaugurated a national form and created a national literary language which was not limited to the abstruse language of books, but included the elemental language of the people. This was a guide to Realism in Russian literature. It must be said, however, that the very genre of the fable inhibited the full flourishing of Realism. For all its correlation to contemporary reality, the fable perceives this reality not in the context of history, but, on the contrary, in its universal significance. This is how it abstracts the manifestations of

146

reality. In other words, despite the veracity of the descriptions in Krylov's fables, they abstract from everyday, specific historical context only isolated typical symptoms and qualities, and display them in their static form and not in their development.

Another factor limiting realism originates from the Enlightenment, namely, the necessity for open didacticism. It must not be forgotten that fable characters did not originate in real life, but started out as personifications and the mouthpieces of moralistic propositions. From the very beginning they were conceived as definite moral theses. This didactic principle is to a large extent overcome in Krylov's fables, enriched as they are with descriptions of everyday life; but nonetheless, they put a brake on their realism. Indeed, if Krylov had decided to leave out the didactic element and make the transition to an empirical portrayal of life, he would have broken out of the very genre of the fable and deprived it of its moral lesson.

The structure of Krylov's fables still had much in common with the didactic Realism of the Enlightenment, but at the same time it was beginning to show the new tendencies of critical Realism and, above all, a national form and a national literary language.

According to Gogol, it was precisely in Krylov's fables that the Realism of Russian literature found its source and acquired its wonderful character types, its verbal vividness, and popular wisdom. He perspicaciously underlined the role of the fable which had seemed to have lost its literary significance by the beginning of the nineteenth century, but was brought back to life in Krylov's works. Belinsky foresaw that "Krylov will lay the road to popular writing for other Russian poets, too."[1] And, indeed, he was the direct forerunner of the Realistic works of Griboedov, Pushkin, and Gogol.

Krylov's contemporary, the poet Wilhelm Küchelbecker, who took part in the Decembrist conspiracy, wrote in his *Diary of an Exile* in 1845:

Last night I dreamt I saw Krylov and Pushkin. I told Krylov that he was Russia's first poet though he did not realize it himself. Then I attempted to propound my thought to Pushkin. I named Griboedov, Pushkin himself, and myself as Kryov's pupils. And now that I am awake I shall say fully consciously that we, that is Griboedov and I, and even Pushkin, are definitely indebted to Krylov for our style. But style is only form, whereas the genres in which we wrote were much higher than the fable, and that is no trifle.[2]

It is significant that in Griboedov's *Woe from Wit* aspects of the language are derived from Krylov: its epigrammatic conciseness, the wealth of conversational intonations, the varying number of iambic feet in the verses depending on the meaning and tone, and the abundance of popular proverbs and verses which later themselves became proverbs.

It goes without saying that it is not enough to list analogous motifs and images to prove the influence of Krylov on any writer. Nonetheless such a list does say something about the affinity of the writers concerned. The fact that Pushkin began his novel-in-verse with a paraphrased line from one of Krylov's fables is not simply chance, but the result of his partiality toward verses closely related to real life—whose very structure was akin to Realism. He preferred the conversational narrative tone and to have his characters unfold their personalities by means of the spoken word. In developing a Russian literary language, the language of Realistic literature, Pushkin continued Krylov's work and extended it to other forms and genres.

When Gogol established his principles of Realistic writing, he was influenced by the way Krylov had evoked the various, vivid, typical characters by means of speech and had endowed each one of them with an individual style. Gogol owes his universal characters, moral teaching, and the vividness of his language to the tradition started by Krylov. We have evidence of the particular interest he took in Krylov's fables from the comprehensive and thoughtful remarks he made about Krylov in an article entitled "What In Fact *Is* the Essence of Russian Poetry and What Are Its Peculiar Features?" He saw Krylov's greatest merit in his ability to expertly handle the language and to "convey the essence of the matter with a powerful word."

Krylov showed the importance of a dialogue or monologue in conveying a realistic picture of a character, who is not only a living being, but also a typical representative of his social or professional milieu. This device became the basis for the in-depth descriptions of Gogol's characters.

Conclusion

The poetry of Nikolay Nekrasov also owes much to Krylov. In his revision of the literary tradition of poetry and search for a popular form of verse, Nekrasov continued the tradition started by Krylov. It is no coincidence that in his *The Wretched Ones* he makes mention of "Krylov's cunning fables." He was attracted by their close ties with folklore, their popular language, and the freedom of their conversational tone. All this influenced him in writing poetry which was deeply national and popular both in form and content. Where Krylov merely alludes to real, earthy features of peasant life, Nekrasov makes them the center of a number of poems. Too, Krylov's reproduction of the conversational tone and the biting humor of his fables were vastly surpassed in Nekrasov's broad panorama of Russian life.

Alexander N. Ostrovsky derived from Krylov's fables not the plot, but the exhortative manner and the general application. Many of his plays have proverbs for titles: *Wolves and Sheep*, *Proverty is No Crime*, *If It's Not Your Sledge Don't Sit in It*, *It Never Rains But It Pours*. The titles alone are allegorical and contain a lesson. As for the characters, despite their realistic portrayal and lifelike, individual characterization, their significance lies in their general social content. The rich, popular language used by most of Ostrovsky's personages seems to come straight from the pages of Krylov's fables.

Also, in the nineteenth century, the Aesopic language of Krylov's fables was used by the great Russian satirist Saltykov-Shchedrin, who was forced to have recourse to its allegorical manner in order to have his ruthless satire published. In addition, he turned to characters from fables to give his own satirical characters general significance. Saltykov-Shchedrin revived many of the characters from Krylov's fables and endowed them with new substance. The stupid, ungrateful pig (*Pig and Truth*), Governor Bear, King Lion, and the titled ass (*Bear as Governor*), the greedy, impudent pike (*The Idealistic Carp*), and the eagle (*Eagle as Patron*)—all these characters from Saltykov-Shchedrin's tales are reincarnations of the ones in Krylov's fables and they retain many features of their original moral make-up. Saltykov's tales are a kind of prose fable the allegorical meaning of which took on a topical character.

Krylov's fables have continued to live on as a genre as well. In the first decade of the twentieth century the writings of a gifted fabulist, Demyan Bedny, appeared. He wrote in the manner of Krylov for the following few decades. He heightened the political tendency of the satire while maintaining the artistic bases of Krylov's fables, the vivid expressiveness of their characters, and their realistic descriptions of everyday life. He also kept to the vividness and accuracy of Krylov's language and its use of popular speech.

The tradition of Krylov's fables is still alive in modern Russian literature in the work of Sergey Mikhalkov, a Soviet fabulist who has revitalized the genre with fresh satirical and moral content.

Krylov's fables were very quickly acclaimed by the world. Many of them were translated into French, Italian, Polish, and other languages during his lifetime. They first appeared in English in 1821 in Sir John Bowring's *Russian Anthology—Specimens of the Russian Poets... with preliminary Remarks and Biographical Notices.* This included the fables *Ass and Nightingale* and *Swan, Pike and Crab.* Bowring, an English merchant and author, seems to have visited Russia in 1810-11 and met Krylov in Petersburg. According to him, Krylov personally gave him a copy of *Ass and Nightingale* for translation before it was published in Russian. In the foreword to the *Russian Anthology,* Bowring dwells on the high standard of fable-writing in Russia, and says that Krylov had published a volume of fables of outstanding style and originality.

The first edition of an English translation—ninety-three fables —appeared in 1869 in London, done by W. R. Ralston, Professor of Russian Language and Slavonic literature.[3] Ralston's translations were published from 1869 to 1883 and included all the original fables in four editions. The third edition was reviewed in the journal *The Academy* (1871) by Ivan Turgenev, who wrote:

Mr. Ralston's translation leaves nothing to be desired in the matter of accuracy or coloring, and the fables which he has added are not amongst the least welcome. The short preface and memoir prefixed to the volume, and the historical and literary notes on some of the fables, have been done conscientiously and *con amore*. It will not be his fault if Krilof [*sic*] does not prove to be thoroughly "naturalized" in England.[4]

This edition made Krylov's fables widely known in England and the English-speaking countries. In 1883, Y. H. Harrison translated 145 fables. In 1942, a London edition came out in a bilingual text. Since then, new English translations of the fables have appeared at regular intervals, both in England and the United States.

Thus, Krylov's fables have become a part of world literature as an eloquent example of Russian national culture alongside the fables of Aesop, Phaedrus, and La Fontaine.

Notes and References

Preface

1. N. V. Gogol', *Polnoe sobranie sochinenii* (Moscow-Leningrad: Izdatelstvo Akademii nauk SSSR, 1952), pp. 391-92. (Note: Publications of the Academy of Science of the USSR will be subsequently abbreviated AN SSSR.)

Chapter One

1. V. F. Kenevich, *Bibliograficheskie i istoricheskie primechaniia k basniam Krylova*, 2nd. ed. (St. Petersburg, 1870), p. 299.

2. Ya. K. Grot, *Trudy* (St. Petersburg, 1901), III, 216.

3. Kenevich, *op. cit.*, p. 301.

4. M. E. Lobanov, *Zhizn' i sochineniia I. A. Krylova* (St. Petersburg, 1847), pp. 2-3.

5. Kenevich, *op. cit.*, pp. 306-7.

6. Lobanov, *op. cit.*, p. 5.

7. *Severnaia pchela*, 1847, No. 282 (St. Petersburg newspaper).

8. *Ibid.*

9. Lobanov, *op. cit.*, p. 66.

10. P. A. Pletnev, *Sochineniia i perepiska* (St. Petersburg, 1885), II, 66.

11. K. N. Batiushkov, *Sochineniia* (St. Petersburg, 1886), III, 53.

12. *Dramaticheskii vestnik*, 1808, No. 8, p. 61.

13. Lobanov, *op. cit.*, p. 55.

14. *Portretnaia i biograficheskaia galeria* (St. Petersburg, 1841), Part II, pp. 4-5.

15. N. I. Grech recalls in his memoirs that in Petersburg Krylov "made a new circle of friends: he met Count A. S. Stroganov and was received at A. N. Olenin's" from *Severnaia Pchela*, 1857, No. 147.

16. *Sovremennik*, May, 1857, pp. 39-40.

17. *Pushkin v vospominaniiakh i rasskazakh sovremennikov* (Leningrad, 1937), p. 321.

18. According to a contemporary, when Gnedich and Krylov were on duty in the Public Library, "a few friends would usually gather there and spend the time of day ... Batiushkov, Milonov, Nikolskii,

Lobanov . . ." *Severnaia pchela*, 1857, No. 159. This, of course, refers to Krylov's first years in the Library.

19. *Publichnaia biblioteka za sto let* (St. Petersburg, 1914), p. 113.

20. *Izvestiia otdeleniia russkogo iazyka i slovesnosti* (Moscow: Akademia Nauk, 1918), XXIII, Book 2, pp. 1-8.

21. I. A. Krylov's *Ukazateli* (Index) are kept in the manuscript section of the Lenin State Library in Moscow.

22. *Russkaia starina*, October, 1847, p. 475.

23. F. A. Oom, *Vospominaniia* (Moscow, 1896), p. 7.

24. Batiushkov, *op. cit.*, I, 146.

25. Lobanov, *op. cit.*, p. 59.

26. A. S. Pushkin, *Sobranie sochinenii*, 10 vols. (Moscow, 1962), VII, 221.

27. P. A. Viazemskii, *Polnoe sobranie sochinenii* (St. Petersburg, 1878), I, 163-64.

28. Pletnev, *op. cit.*, II, 92.

29. Pushkin, *op. cit.*, VI, 15.

30. K. A. Polevoi, from notes in, by N. A. Polevoi: *Materialy po istorii russkoi literatury i zhurnalistiki 30-kh godov* (Leningrad: Izdatelstvo Pisatelei v Leningrade, 1934), pp. 208-9.

31. A. I. Herzen, *Sobranie sochinenii*, 30 vols. (Moscow: AN SSSR, 1954-1961), VII, 209.

32. The meetings at Zhukovskii's house with the participation of Krylov, Batiushkov, Karamzin, Viazemskii and others in 1810-1820 are described by Zhukovskii's biographer, K. Zeydlits, *Zhizn' i poeziia V. A. Zhukovskogo* (St. Petersburg, 1883), p. 127.

33. Pletnev, *op. cit.*, II, 81.

34. I. A. Krylov, *Polnoe sobranie sochinenii* (Moscow, 1946), III, 358. Henceforth referred to as Krylov, *Polnoe sobranie. . . .*

35. I. S. Turgenev, *Sobranie sochinenii*, 12 vols. (Moscow, 1956), X, 329.

36. *Privetstviia, govorennye I. A. Krylovu v den' ego rozhdeniia i sovershivshevosia piatidesiatiletiia ego literaturnoi deiatel'nosti* (St. Petersburg, 1838).

37. Krylov, *Polnoe sobranie . . .* , III, 380.

Chapter Two

1. A. N. Radishchev, *Polnoe sobranie sochinenii* (Moscow-Leningrad: AN SSSR, 1938), I, 127.

2. M. Gorkii, *Isotoriia russkoi literatury* (Moscow, 1939), p. 14.

3. Krylov himself provided the grounds for this interpretation in a light-hearted comment on his youthful tragedy: "In my youth,"

he told Lobanov, "I wrote about everything under the sun—all I needed was paper and ink. I also wrote a tragedy [*Philomela*]. It was printed in *Russkii teatr* in the same issue as Kniazhnin's *Vadim*, and disappeared together with it. And I am glad it did; it had nothing to recommend it. It was one of my first attempts of long ago" (Lobanov, *op. cit.*, p. 9).

4. *Zritel'*, June, 1792, p. 120.

5. Krylov, *Polnoe sobranie . . .* , I, 399.

6. D. I. Zavalishin, *Zapiski* (St. Petersburg, 1904), I, 181.

7. Krylov, *Sochineniia v dvukh tomakh* (Moscow, 1955), II, 301. Henceforth, all quotations from Krylov's works, unless specified, come from this publication, with the volume and page marked in the text, except for the fables translated by Bernard Pares, which give the volume and number of the complete edition of the fables.

8. The question of Krylov's authorship of *Pochta dukhov* has frequently been disputed. But a careful analysis of the content and composition of the letters leaves no room for doubt on that score. See N. L. Stepanov, I. A. Krylov, *Zhizn' i tvorchestvo* (Moscow, 1958), p. 84.

9. V. G. Belinskii, *Polnoe sobranie sochinenii* (Moscow: AN SSSR, 1953-1959), VIII, 585.

Chapter Three

1. Lobanov, *op. cit.*, pp. 48-49.
2. *Tsvetnik*, 1810, VIII, pp. 117-18.
3. F. F. Vigel', *Zapiski* (Moscow, 1891-1893), Part VI, p. 15.
4. Pushkin, *op. cit.*, VI, 15.
5. Gogol', *op. cit.*, VIII, 392.
6. Belinskii, *op. cit.*, VIII, 571.
7. *Ibid.*, p. 570.
8. Gogol', *op. cit.*, VIII, 392-93.
9. Belinskii, *op. cit.*, VIII, 574.
10. *Ibid.*, IV, 151.
11. See A. G. Tseitlin's article, "Krylov i Lafonten" in the collection, *I. A. Krylov: Issledovaniia i materialy*, ed. by D. D. Blagoi and N. L. Brodskii (Moscow, 1947), pp. 187-208.
12. Belinskii, *op. cit.*, IV, 150-51.
13. *Ibid.*, VIII, 114.

Chapter Four

1. Belinskii, *op. cit.*, VIII, 575-76.
2. Herzen, *op. cit.*, VII, 95.

3. Alexander A. Bestuzhev-Marlinskii, *Sochineniia v dvukh tomakh* (Moscow, 1958), II, 530.

4. "*Iz pisem i pokazanii dekabristov,*" *pod redaktsiei A. Borozdina* (St. Petersburg, 1906), p. 40.

5. *Vosstanie dekabristov* (Leningrad, 1927), II, 166.

6. Kenevich, *op. cit.*, p. 84.

7. *Severnaia pchela*, 1845, No. 9, p. 65.

8. A. A. Potebnia. *Iz lektsii po teorii slovesnosti* (Kharkov, 1894), p. 75.

Chapter Five

1. Belinskii, *op. cit.*, IV, 148.

2. *Basni Aesopa* (Moscow, 1968), p. 100.

3. Jean de La Fontaine, *Fables* (Paris, 1923), p. 8.

4. G. E. Lessing, *Gesammelte Werke* (Berlin, 1955), IV, 72.

5. *Russkaia basnia* (Leningrad, 1949), p. 48.

6. *Trudy obshchestva liubitelei russkoi slovesnosti pri Moskovskom universitete* (Moscow, 1812), Part I, p. 103.

7. Belinskii, *op. cit.*, VIII, 573.

8. La Fontaine, *Fables* (Paris, 1929), p. 10.

9. Belinskii, *op. cit.*, IV, 149.

10. Potebnia, *op. cit.*, pp. 74-75.

11. Ivan I. Khemnitser, *Polnoe sobranie stikhotvorenii* (Moscow-Leningrad, 1963), p. 97.

12. *Vestnik Evropy*, 1812, No. 4, p. 390.

13. Alexander E. Izmailov, *Basni i skazki* (St. Petersburg, 1826), Part 3, p. 19.

Chapter Six

1. Belinskii, *op. cit.*, VIII, 575.

2. V. K. Trediakovskii, *Sochineniia* (St. Petersburg, 1849), I, 21.

3. Potebnia, *op. cit.*, p. 26.

4. *Sovremennik*, 1838, IX, 57.

5. Belinskii, *op. cit.*, IV, 149.

6. G. W. F. Hegel, Sochineniia, "*Lektsii po estetike*" (Moscow, 1938), Vol. XII, Book I, p. 398.

7. A. E. Izmailov, *op. cit.*, III, 66.

8. V. I. Pokrovskii (comp.), *I. A. Krylov: Ego zhizn' i sochineniia. Sbornik istoriko-literaturnykh statei* (Moscow, 1911), 3rd. ed., p. 153.

9. Pushkin, *op. cit.*, VI, 275.

10. A. Nikitenko, *O basniakh Krylova v khudozhestvennom otno-*

shenii. Sbornik statei, chitannykh v Otdelenii russkogo iazyka i slovesnosti Akademii nauk (St. Petersburg, 1868), VI, 53.

11. Belinskii, *op. cit.*, IV, 150-51.

12. Gogol', *op. cit.*, VI, 169.

13. L. I. Timofeev, *Ocherki teorii i istorii russkogo stikha* (Moscow, 1958), p. 350.

14. Vassily A. Zhukovskii, *Sochineniia* (St. Petersburg, 1878), VII, 349.

15. For Krylov's use of sound in his fables, see the paper by the Italian, Pachini-Savoi, *L'instrumentazione musicale nelle favole di I. A. Krylov, Annali* (Naples, 1958).

16. Lobanov, *op. cit.*, p. 51.

17. Gogol', *op. cit.*, VIII, 394-95.

18. Viazemskii, *op. cit.*, I, 157.

19. V. V. Vinogradov, *Yazyk i stil' basen Krylova—Izvestiia Otdeleniia literatury i iazyka Akademii nauk SSSR* (Moscow, 1945), 1st. ed., IV, 35.

20. *Ibid.*, p. 48.

Conclusion

1. Belinskii, *op. cit.*, VIII, 114.

2. V. K. Küchelbecker, *Dnevnik* (Leningrad, 1929), pp. 303-4.

3. W. R. Ralston, *Krilof and his Fables* (London, 1883).

4. Turgenev, *op. cit.*, XI, 205.

Selected Bibliography

PRIMARY SOURCES

In Russian:

Basni v deviati knigakh. St. Petersburg: 1843.
Polnoe sobranie sochinenii I. A. Krylova. S biografiei ego, napisannoi P. A. Pletnevym. 3 vols. St. Petersburg: 1847.
Polnoe sobranie sochinenii I. A. Krylova. Pod redaktsiei V. V. Kalasha. 4 vols. St. Petersburg: 1905 and 1918.
Polnoe sobranie sochinenii I. A. Krylova. Pod redaktsiei D. Bednogo, D. Brodskogo, i N. Stepanova. 3 vols. Moscow: Gosudarstvennoe izdatel'stvo khudozhestvennoi literatury, 1944-1946.
Sochineniia I. A. Krylova v dvukh tomakh. Pod redaktsiei N. L. Stepanova. Moscow: Gosudarstvennoe izdatel'stvo khudozhestvennoi literatury, 1955.
Basni. Pod redaktsiei A. P. Mogilianskogo. Moscow-Leningrad: Izdatel'stvo Akademii nauk SSSR, 1956.
Basni, proza, p'esy, stikhi. Pod redaktsiei A. A. Develia. Leningrad: Lenizdat, 1970.
I. A. Kryloff. Edited, with introduction, notes, and vocabulary by Y. H. Freese. London: 1917. (Fables in Russian; introduction in English; Russian-English vocabulary.)

In English:

Krilof and his Fables. Translated from the Russian by W. R. J. Ralston. London: 1869. Fourth Edition, London: 1883.
Original Fables. Translated by I. Henry Harrison. London: 1883.
Kriloff's Fables. Translated from the Russian into English by C. Fillingham Coxwell. New York: E. P. Dutton, 1920.
Krylov's Fables. Translated into English Verse. Preface by Bernard Pares. London: 1926.
Krylov's Fables. Translated into English Verse. Preface by Bernard Pares. London: 1927.
Russian Fables of Ivan Krylov. Verse translation by Bernard Pares, Russian and English texts. Harmondsworth, Middlesex and New York: Penguin Books, 1942.

159

Fables from Russia. Adapted by Stella Mead. London: Oxford University Press, 1943.

Fifteen Fables of Krylov. Translated by Guy Daniels. New York: Macmillan, 1965.

SECONDARY SOURCES

In Russian:

BABINTSEV, S. M. *I. A. Krylov. Ocherk ego izdatel'skoi i bibliotechnoi deiatel'nosti* Moscow: Izdanie Vsesoiuznoi knizhnoi palaty, 1955.

BELINSKII, VISSARION G. *O Krylove.* Moscow: Gosizdat khudozhestvennoi literatury, 1944.

DESNITSKII, A. V. *Krylov-basnopisets. Etiudy o tvorchestve I. A. Krylova.* Leningrad: Uchonye zapiski Leningradskogo pedagogicheskogo instituta imeni A. I. Gertsena, 1937, Vol. III, 7-54.

DURYLIN, S. N. *I. A. Krylov. Kratkii ocherk zhizni i tvorchestva.* Moscow: Gosizdat khudozhestvennoi literatury, 1944.

KENEVICH, V. F. *Bibliograficheskie i istoricheskie primechaniia k basniam Krylova.* 2nd. ed. St. Petersburg: 1869.

KRYLOV, I. A. *Issledovaniia i materialy. Sbornik statei Instituta mirovoi literatury imeni A. M. Gor'kogo Akademii nauk SSSR.* Moscow: 1947.

LOBANOV, M. E. *Zhizn' i sochineniia I. A. Krylova.* St. Petersburg: 1847.

PUSHKIN, ALEXANDER S. *O predislovii g. Lemonte k perevodu basen Krylova. Sobranie sochinenii v 10 tomakh.* Vol. VI. Moscow: Gosizdat khudozhestvennoi literatury, 1944.

SERGEEV, IVAN. *I. A. Krylov.* In series: *Velikie russkie liudi.* Moscow: "Molodaia gvardiia," 1945.

SHAGINIAN, M. S. *I. A. Krylov.* Erevan: Armianskoe gosudarstvennoe izdatel'stvo, 1944.

STEPANOV, N. L. *I. A. Krylov. Zhizn' i tvorchestvo.* Moscow: Gosizdat khudozhestvennoi literatury, 1958.

————. *Krylov.* In series: *Zhizn' zamechatel'nykh liudei.* 2nd. ed. Moscow: "Molodaya Gvardya," 1969.

————. *Masterstvo Krylova-basnopistsa.* Moscow: Izdatel'stvo "Sovetskii pisatel'," 1956.

VINOGRADOV, V. V. *Iazyk i stil' basen Krylova.* Moscow: Izvestiia AN SSSR. Otdelenie literatury i iazyka, 1945. 1st. ed., Vol. IV, 24-52.

ZAPADOV, A. V. "I. A. Krylov." Vol I. of *Russkie dramaturgi.* 3 vols. Moscow-Leningrad: Izdatel'stvo "Iskusstvo," 1951.

ZAPADOV, A. V. AND GOFMAN, V. A. "Krylov." *Istoriia russkoi literatury.* Moscow-Leningrad: AN SSSR, 1941, V, 235-66.

General Reference Works on Krylov:

BABINTSEV, S. M. *I. A. Krylov. Ukazatel' ego proizvedenii i literatury o nem. K stoletiiu so dnia smerti, 1844-1944.* Leningrad-Moscow: Izdatel'stvo "Iskusstvo," 1945.
Istoriia russkoi literatury XIX veka. Bibliograficheskii ukazatel' pod redaktsiei K. D. Muratovoi. Moscow-Leningrad: AN SSSR, 1962.

English-Russian Appendix
of the Fables Mentioned in the Text

Book I

1	Crow and Fox	Vorona i Lisitsa
2	Oak and Reed	Dub i Trost
3	The Village Band	Muzy Kanty
4	Crow and Hen	Vorona i Kuritsa
5	A Little Box	Larchik
6	Frog and Bullock	Lyagushka i Vol
7	The Dainty Spinster	Razborchivaya Nevesta
8	Parnassus	Parnas
13	Wolf and Lamb	Volk i Yagnyonok
15	Tom-Tit	Sinitsa
16	The Ass	Osyol
17	Miss Monkey and Her Spectacles	Martyshka i Ochki
21	The Godless Tribe	Bezbozhniki

Book II

1	The Frogs Ask for a King	Lyagushki, prosyashchie Tsarya
3	Statesman and Thinker	Velmozha i Filosof
4	The Plague of the Beasts	Mor zverey
5	Dogs' Friendship	Sobachya druzhba
6	Sharing Up	Razdel
8	Wolf in the Kennels	Volk na psarne
9	The Brook	Ruchey
10	Fox and Marmot	Lisitsa i Surok
12	Gadfly and Ant	Strekoza i Muravey
13	The Liar	Lzhets
14	Eagle and Bee	Oryol i Pchela
15	The Hare A-Hunting	Zayats na lovle
16	Pike and Cat	Shchuka i Kot
17	Wolf and Cuckoo	Volk i Kukushka
19	Old Mat and His Man	Krestyanin i Rabotnik
20	A Train of Carts	Oboz
21	The Raven Chick	Voronyonok
22	Elephant as Governor	Slon na voevodstve
23	Ass and Nightingale	Osyol i Solovey

Nikolay L. Stepanov

Professor Nikolay L. Stepanov, Doctor of Philology, has been associated with the Gorky Institute of World Literature of the USSR Academy of Sciences in Moscow since 1943. He began his research at the Institute of Russian Literature (Pushkin House) in Leningrad in 1934. He is the author of many works on Russian literature and literary criticism of the eighteenth and nineteenth centuries, including monographs on the works of Pushkin, Gogol, and Nikolay Nekrasov.

He has written the following works on Krylov and on the history of Russian fables: *The Art of the Fabulist Krylov* (1956), *I. A. Krylov: Life and Works* (1958), *Krylov: a biography* (1969), and *Krylov Fables* (1969). A number of his works have been translated into foreign languages.

Index

Aesop (-ic), 28, 30, 71, 75, 76, 86, 94, 95, 96, 97, 98, 102, 110, 111, 124, 130, 149, 151

Alexander I, Tsar, 75, 77-81, 84-85, 88

Alfieri, Count Vittorio, 30

Arakcheev, Count Alexis, 75, 78, 80

Batyushkov, Konstantin N., 22, 26, 28, 32, 56, 57

Bedny, Demyan, 150

Belinsky, Vissarion G., 22, 30, 31, 53, 59, 68-69, 71, 74, 75, 77, 84, 87, 94, 100, 101, 109, 111, 133, 147

Beseda Lyubiteley Russkogo Slova; *see* Society of the Lovers of the Russian Word

Bestuzhev, Alexander A., 31, 77, 81

Boileau, Nicolas, 16

Borodino, Battle of, 61

Bowring, Sir John, 150

Bryullov, K., 34

Bulgarin, Faddey V., 92, 115

Bystrov, I., 27

Caligula, his horse, 51

Captain's Daughter, The (Pushkin), 13

Catherine II, 20, 54

Chichagov, Admiral Pavel V., 106

Chulkov, Mikhail D., 35

Classicism, Classicist(s), 23, 24, 29, 35, 37, 40, 41, 42, 46, 56, 70, 77, 90, 100, 109, 137, 141, 145, 146

Contrat social, Le (Rousseau), 50

Decembrists, the, 22, 23, 31, 43, 75, 77, 81

Delvig, Baron Anton A., 26, 27

Derzhavin, Gavriil R., 22, 25, 35, 56

Diable Boiteux, Le (Lesage), 49

Dialogues of the Gods (Lucian), 51

Diary of an Exile (Küchelbecker), 147-48

Diderot, Denis, 19, 36

Dmitrevsky, I. A., 18

Dmitriev, I. I., 21, 57, 58, 59, 91, 100, 138

Dramatichesky vestnik (Dramatic Herald), 23

Eighteenth Century, The (Radishchev), 36-37

Emin, Fyodor A., 46

Encyclopaedists, The, 19

Enlightenment, The, 17, 18, 19, 35, 36, 37, 38, 46, 47, 48, 49, 50, 51, 52, 57, 64, 65, 67, 99, 102, 147

Erasmus, Desiderius, 53

Evgeny Onegin (Pushkin), 139

fable, development of the, 94-98

fable, the Russian, 57-58, 94, 96-97, 98-100, 124

Ferguson, Adam, 36

Fille, La (La Fontaine), 69

Fonvizin, Denis, 15, 19, 22, 35, 37, 38, 39, 52, 81

Free Society of Lovers of Russian Literature, 31

French Revolution, the, 19, 36, 49, 67, 88, 89

Gallomania, Russian, 36, 44-45, 51

Gellert, Christian Fürchtegott, 99, 103, 110, 114

German influence in Russia, 21, 42-43

169

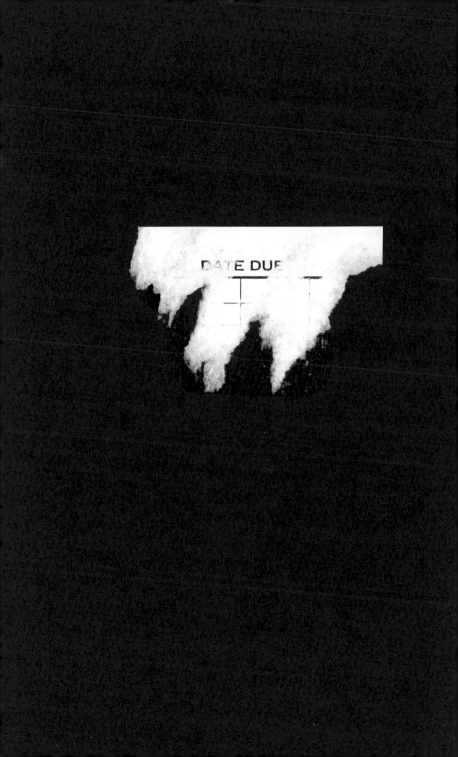

DATE DUE